Logos Immanuel
Word: God with Us

By

Charles F. Marshall

Book

Celeste Press
Atlanta, Georgia

Logos Immanuel
Word: God with us
Book Two

*To the Glory of God who makes all
things possible*

MESSAGE FROM THE AUTHOR:

Dear Reader,

Writing this devotional has been one of the most enriching blessings to which I am very grateful. The genesis of this project started out of sharing daily messages with coworkers each day. Persons would come by my cubicle or call me to ask for a word for the day. As I got on the elevator each day, someone would ask me for a word for the day. By the grace of God, I was able to share a word with them.

In the spirit of efficiency, I decided to simply email a copy of a word for the day to the many people who I had come in contact with. Having recently completed a Master of Divinity Degree from the Interdenominational Theological Center in Atlanta, Georgia, I have a great deal to share to whoever God sent my way and would listen. It is through this platform of sharing that God has allowed the creation of this devotional to take place.

I hope that it blesses you and the people in your life. God's word is living and breathing and even transforming. I've seen how the word of God transformed choirs, usher boards, steward boards, trustees, pastors, and even myself. Our biggest obstacle is ourselves. If you are blessed by something in this book, please share it with a friend.

Even though many of the texts referenced from the Holy Bible were written over thousands of years ago, they are contemporary, practical applications for today. Take 15-20 minutes in your day to spend in reflection. Use the spaces available to write what you are thinking at the time. Come back later and see what you thought. If you are blessed, share it with someone you love. If you find time, write me to tell me.

In God's Service,
Charles F. Marshall, III

Mailing Address :

Rev. Charles F. Marshall, III
PO BOX 55039
Atlanta, GA 30308

Table of Contents

1. Never Enough

Haggai 1:6-7 Ye have sown much, and bring in little; ye eat, but ye have not enough; ye drink, but ye are not filled with drink; ye clothe you, but there is none warm; and he that earneth wages earneth wages [to put it] into a bag with holes. Thus saith the LORD of hosts; Consider your ways.

There is a family that is emulated by so many people in neighborhoods around the world. This family is called the Jones family.   No one knows how the Jones family found the palm tree to put in their front yard, but several people in the neighbor bought a palm tree for their front yard after seeing the palm in the Jones family yard.   No one knows how the Jones family acquired the new brick mailbox at the end of their drive way, but several people installed brick mailboxes after seeing the Jones family new mailbox.   No one knew why Ray Ray Jones had to wear a gold tooth in his mouth, but kids at the bus stop started wearing gold colored grills after seeing Ray Ray's shiny tooth. Some people say they live from paycheck to paycheck and it seems that "ends never meet". It's almost like putting your paycheck in a bag with holes.   At the turn of the century, people had small closets which contained a dress outfit, a work outfit, and shoes. Now most people have to choose what to wear from their walk in closets and they still will say they don't have enough. If an outfit is on sale, most will buy another outfit even if they don't need it. When is enough enough? If we are guilty of this, maybe we need to "consider our ways." Have a Great Day!

Prayer
Lord, thank you for you for all your blessings. Thank you for life, health, peace, and hope. Help me to appreciate all that you do for me and my loved ones. Amen.

Personal Reflections

Date: _____

Thoughts:_____

_____

_____

_____

_____

_____

This Day's Objective:_____

_____

_____

_____

_____

2. Church and State

Luke 20:25 And he said unto them, Render therefore unto Caesar the things which be Caesar's, and unto God the things which be God's.

The people of God and the government have coexisted as far back as history records. Many times these are the same people. The Old Testament records the story of how Moses, Esther, and many others were children of God but serve in a leading and influential role in government. Church leaders have been advisors to many kings and presidents. Some church leaders actually serve or have served in Government like Rev. Floyd Flake, Rev. Shirley Caesar, and even Rev. Andrew Young. Yet, today there is a cry to separate church and state and also a cry to put the church back in state. Where the actual line of demarcation should exist is still being debated so there will always be tension. Fortunately, the persecution that existed for Christians throughout history no longer exists. One thing that is in agreement throughout the ages is that the voice of God transcends all governments and powers. Jesus reminds us in Luke 20:25, that the things that are God's have merit and weight just as government matters have weight. There is even record that Jesus had one of the disciples to go to fetch money from a fish's mouth to pay taxes or tribute (Matthew 17:24-27). Governments exist for the people. The people exist for God. All things work together for them that love the Lord and are called according to His purpose.(Romans 8:28) Say a prayer for the church and for the government.   Have a great day!

Prayer
God, Bless the government; bless the people; bless the church; and bless me.
Amen

Personal Reflections

Date: _____

Thoughts:_____

_____

_____

_____

_____

_____

This Day's Objective:_____

_____

_____

_____

_____

_____

3. Loosed To Serve

Luke 19:33-34 And as they were loosing the colt, the owners thereof said unto them, Why loose ye the colt? And they said, The Lord hath need of him.

Helen Adams Keller was born full of sight and hearing in Tuscumbia, a small northwest Alabama town, to Captain Arthur and Kate Adams Keller. In February 1882, at the age of nineteen months old, Helen became gravely ill and became deaf and blind. Alexander Graham Bell suggested that the Kellers seek Michael Anagnos, director of the Perkins Institution and Massachusetts Asylum for the Blind to request a teacher for Helen. Anne Sullivan became Helen's teacher. It was Anne who taught Helen to speak with her hands and eventually write with ordinary letters and then with Braille letters. Helen entered Radcliff College becoming the first deaf and blind person to attend an institution of higher learning. Helen later said in her own words "The public must learn that the blind man is neither genius nor a freak nor an idiot. He has a mind that can be educated, a hand which can be trained, ambitions which it is right for him to strive to realize, and it is the duty of the public to help him make the best of himself so that he can win light through work." Keller devoted much of her later life to raise funds for the American Foundation for the Blind. She died in 1968, passing away at the age of 87 in her Easton, Connecticut home. Every Child of God is like Helen in the sense that God allows us to grow to help others. We are saved to "Go ye therefore and teach all nations". Like the colt that was loosed to serve Jesus, we are saved and grow in our relationship with God to be a light to others. There's a wise proverb that says "We are blessed to bless others."

 Have a great day!

Prayer
Dear God, Help me to become all that you have created me to be and to be a blessing for someone else. Amen

Personal Reflections

Date: _____

Thoughts:_____

_____

_____

_____

_____

This Day's Objective:_____

_____

_____

_____

_____

_____

4. Merciful and Gracious

Psalm 103:8 The LORD [is] merciful and gracious, slow to anger, and plenteous in mercy.

On the annual road trip from Rochester, New York to the new vacation destination, Ft. Walton Beach, Florida, time in the car involves a multitude of activities for the passengers. Since everyone left at 4:00 am in the morning, the first few hours were relatively quiet as everyone except the driver took naps using the blankets and pillows that they hastingly grabbed as they packed the van at 3:00 a.m. in the morning. At about 8:00 a.m. as the van moved through the state of Maryland, little Johnny had awakened and began chewing gum. At about 8:10 a.m., little Johnny began to blow bubbles with chewing gum and make a popping noises, yet the driver said nothing. At about 8:15 a.m., little Johnny began to tap the window in between popping the bubbles, and driver said "stop Johnny". Little Johnny stopped tapping the window and popping bubbles. At about 8:20 a.m., little Johnny started popping bubbles again but this time he started tapping his sister's head. The driver and his sister said "Stop Johnny!!!!". Johnny stopped, but repeated the cycle again until the driver handed Johnny a napkin and said "spit the gum in the napkin and give it back to me". Johnny is like so many of us adults when it comes to being obedient to the will of God. Psalm 103:8 reminds us that God loves us in spite of ourselves. God is merciful and gracious and even slow to anger. Yet, we continue to "pop gum" or live out of God's will. This verse never says that God won't get angry, but God is patient. At some point we need to "spit the gum out" or live according to God's will rather than suffer the consequences. In the old days, the consequences from parents used to be a swift back hand for disobedience. We should not provoke God to anger, we should be obedient to God's will. Within God's will, Psalm 23 reminds us that "Goodness and Mercy" shall follow us all the days of our lives.

HAVE A GREAT DAY!

Prayer
God, Thank you for your mercy and your grace. Amen

Personal Reflections

Date: _____

Thoughts:_____

_____

_____

_____

_____

_____

_____

This Day's Objective:_____

_____

_____

_____

_____

_____

_____

5. Christian Sheep

John 10:27 My sheep hear my voice, and I know them, and they follow me:

On my annual summer trip to visit my grandmother, there was a chore called rounding up the cows. Basically, we were supposed to go to some point near the cow pen where the cows are normally held, and begin screaming this high pitched call that sounded like "Woo". The cows were supposed to answer and eventually start coming to the cow pen from deep within the woods in the cow pasture. After several minutes of this calling and the cows don't come, my cousins and I would have to go into the woods and find the cows and lead them back to the cow pen. On the other hand, my grandmother would sometimes come to the cow pen, and call for the cows and the cows would answer and begin their journey back to the cow pen. We discovered that the cows knew her voice. Those of us, who call ourselves Christians, hear the voice of Christ in our daily living. Not only do we hear Christ, we follow Christ's instruction and we believe that Christ knows us by name. That's where a "personal relationship" with Christ comes from. There is an old hymn that reflects this sentiment: "I come to the garden alone while the dew is still on the roses. The voice I hear falling on my ear, the Son of God discloses. And He walks with me and He talks with me, and He tells me I am his own, and the joy we share as we tarry there none other has ever known."

Have a great day!

Prayer
O God, Help me to hear your voice. Spirit of the Living God fall fresh on me. Make me. Mold me. Cleanse me. Guide me. Amen

Personal Reflections

Date: _____

Thoughts:_____

_____

_____

_____

_____

_____

This Day's Objective:_____

_____

_____

_____

_____

_____

6. Morning Prayer

Psalm 5:3 My voice shalt thou hear in the morning, O LORD; in the morning will I direct [my prayer] unto thee, and will look up.

There is an old saying that early bird gets the worm. Most people feel that getting worms is not a priority in their book. However, an older gentleman showed me a trick with regards to getting worms to go fishing. We both got up a very early in the morning at the crack of day. We began to pull back the dew filled leaves and there lay clumps of earth worms.

Consequently, we found a bucket of worms to go fishing. There is something special about getting up early to do things before the day gets busy. While God hears us at any time of the day, there is something special about time with God in the morning. Psalm 55:17 says "Evening, and morning, and at noon, will I pray, and cry aloud: and he shall hear my voice". In the morning, there are fewer distractions and we are better positioned to hear God's voice. Take time in the morning before the kids get up, before the phone calls start, before the television is turned on, and even before breakfast to find time with God. See what a difference it makes.

Have a great day!

Prayer

Dear God, bless me and all those that I meet this day with your favor. Thank you for the new mercies I see this day. In the name of Jesus, Amen.

Personal Reflections

Date: _____

Thoughts:_____

_____

_____

_____

_____

_____

_____

This Day's Objective:_____

_____

_____

_____

_____

_____

_____

7. God's Got Our Back

Genesis 31:49-50 And Mizpah; for he said, The LORD watch between me and thee, when we are absent one from another. If thou shalt afflict my daughters, or if thou shalt take [other] wives beside my daughters, no man [is] with us; see, God [is] witness betwixt me and thee.

There are some people that can not be trusted. Have you had someone that you had to watch everything you say around them because when it is repeated, it never sounds like what you originally stated?   Or have you ever had to hide certain things like cologne, perfume, money, books, shoes, or even clothes when a certain person visits because things always come up missing when that person leaves? No matter how much we love a person, there are some people that are very difficult to trust. Jacob and Laban came to terms with their inability to trust one another. Laban turned to God and asked God to watch between him and Jacob because there were no other witnesses.   God sees all and God knows all. While we ask God to watch over the time we are apart, sometimes we just have to manage our time and presence with people we can't trust. There is a saying that you feed a dog with a long handle spoon so you don't get bit.   Jesus reminds us in Matthew 13:30 that we still must get along with people that we don't trust: "Let both grow together until the harvest: and in the time of harvest I will say to the reapers, Gather ye together first the tares, and bind them in bundles to burn them: but gather the wheat into my barn." Jesus will do the separating when He returns. HAVE A GREAT DAY!

Prayer

O God, Thank for your provision and your protection. Right now, continue to be my shepherd and protect me from the things I see and can not see that may harm me. In Jesus' Name, Amen.

Personal Reflections

Date: _____

Thoughts:_____

_____

_____

_____

_____

_____

This Day's Objective:_____

.

_____

_____

_____

_____

_____

8. It Takes Faith

Hebrew 11:6 But without faith [it is] impossible to please [him]: for he that cometh to God must believe that he is, and [that] he is a rewarder of them that diligently seek him.

A person who goes fishing has to utilize faith to cast into to the deep to catch fish.   The process of fishing is simple but complex. A person, equipped with bait, a fishing pole, a fishing line, a hook, and a container to put the fish, goes to a body of water such as a lake, a pond, a river, a stream, or even an ocean. To take all this stuff to a body of a water means that the person is expecting to do something with them. Upon arrival to the body of water, the person looks at the body of water and sees nothing but water. Sometimes the water is calm and sometimes the water is choppy. Sometimes the water is noisy with motion and other times it is quiet with absolutely no movement, yet the objective is get fish from this body of water.   You can't see below the surface to see if there are even fish present, but something within tells you that there are fish under the surface.   So the person, out of faith, takes his pole and attaches his fishing line, hook and bait. The person believes that if he can just get his line in the water with the bait, he will be able to catch a fish. Once the person connects with the water, then fish do their thing. The fish tugs the bait which tugs the line which tugs the pole which tugs the person, and the person knows to respond by tugging the pole and fish is caught. God expects us to seek him by faith. Equipped with our fishing tackle --Holy Scriptures, prayer, and the Holy Spirit--

we seek God turning from our wicked ways in a humbling way. God in turns hears our prayer and tugs on our line to let us know he heard us. Charles Albert Tindley expressed how our faith is renewed as we seek him through the words of his hymn: *Beams of heaven as I go through the wilderness below. Guide my feet in peaceful ways. Turn my midnights into days. When in the darkness I would grope, faith always sees a star of hope and soon from all life's grief and danger I shall be free someday.* Timothy Wright just says "trouble don't *last always.*"

Have a great day!

Prayer

God who created the heavens and the earth, increase my faith. Help me to grow closer to you so that I may please you. In the name of Jesus, Amen.

Personal Reflections

Date: _____

Thoughts:_____

_____

_____

_____

_____

This Day's Objective:_____

_____

_____

_____

_____

_____

_____

9. When Elevated To High Places

Genesis 41:39-41 And Pharaoh said unto Joseph, Forasmuch as God hath shewed thee all this, [there is] none so discreet and wise as thou [art]: Thou shalt be over my house, and according unto thy word shall all my people be ruled: only in the throne will I be greater than thou. And Pharaoh said unto Joseph, See, I have set thee over all the land of Egypt.

Frederick Baily was born a slave in February 1818 on Holmes Hill Farm near Easton, Maryland. As a child he was fed cornmeal mush that was placed in a trough and shared by the other children who made homemade spoons from oyster shells to eat the mush. Growing up, Frederick was sent to Baltimore and was read the bible by the mistress. He asked if she would teach him to read but was denied. He later learned the alphabet on his own and made friends with poor white children he met on errands and used them as teachers. He paid for his reading lessons with pieces of bread. After learning to read and write, Frederick bought a copy of "The Columbian Orator", a collection of speeches and essays dealing with liberty, democracy, and courage. In 1838, Frederick changed his name to Frederick Douglass after a character in the book, "The Lady of Lake" in order to elude slave catchers. He became one of the foremost leaders of the abolitionist movement which fought to end slavery within the United States prior to the Civil War. Douglass served as advisor to President Abraham Lincoln during the Civil War and fought for the adoption of constitutional amendments that guaranteed voting rights and civil liberties for blacks. Douglass, like Joseph in the biblical account, was a member an oppressed group who found favor in the eyes of God. God equipped them to be elevated to high political places not just for their own glory and well being, but to serve as a voice for their people. Today, just like many of the historical figures of the past, those people who are placed in places of affluence and influence are placed there to represent and speak on behalf of their people and to ultimately serve the will of God. It is God who gives the ability to be wise and to lead and it is God who places men and women in high places.   We must be true to our God and our people like James Weldon Johnson warns in his song, "Lift Every Voice and Sing": "God of our weary years, God of our silent tears, Thou Who hast brought us thus far on the way; Thou Who hast by Thy might, led us into the light, Keep us forever in the path, we pray. Lest our feet stray from the places, our God, where we met Thee. Lest our hearts, drunk with the wine of the world, we forget Thee. Shadowed beneath Thy hand, may we forever stand, True to our God, true to our native land."

 Have a Great Day!

Prayer
O God, Thank you for being with us to this point in our lives. Help us to remember you as you elevate us in life.   Help us to bless others as you have blessed us. May we be pleasing in your sight, our God, our redeemer. In the name of Jesus.

Personal Reflections

Date: _____

Thoughts:_____

_____

_____

_____

_____

This Day's Objective:_____

_____

_____

_____

_____

_____

_____

10. Church Rock

Matthew 16:18 And I say also unto thee, That thou art Peter, and upon this rock I will build my church; and the gates of hell shall not prevail against it.

Nothing stirs up the emotions of people like issues related to the church. On Earth there is a constant tension between good and evil; between those in the church and those outside the church. Since the establishment of the church, people involved in the church were either persecuted or were the persecutors, or just the complacent inhabitants. Today, most news stories related to the church involve some scandal or some controversial area related to a church position. Very seldom do you hear of how the church gives hope, provides help, nurtures, loves, and even lifts people out their circumstances. On June 15, 1520, Pope Leo X threatened in the papal bull, Exsurge Domine, to excommunicate Martin Luther for his revolutionary stand to reform some of the bad practices that had been practiced by leaders of the church. As history played out, it was Martin Luther who made significant contributions to the church such as a bible in the tongue of the people, German, which helped to standardize the German language. Today, the church takes on many forms, but what holds true is that Christ and the church has continued to make their presence in the life all people. Even centuries later, an African American man from Georgia named Martin Luther King Jr called the church and government to accountability for how African Americans were being treated all over the United States of America. Yes, there are many areas that could use some improvement in the church, but what holds true is the gates of hell still have to give way for the will of God. The Church is still doing great things. What is the will of God? The apostle Paul says (Romans 12:2) And be not conformed to this world: but be ye transformed by the renewing of your mind, that ye may prove what [is] that good, and acceptable, and perfect, will of God. Renew your mind and you will build the church in you on a rock that will stand the test of time and adversity!

 Have a great day!

Prayer
O God, Thank you for your church. Continue to bless your church and bless us to be a blessing to your church. In Jesus' Name, Amen.

Personal Reflections

Date: _____

Thoughts:_____

_____

_____

_____

_____

_____

_____

This Day's Objective:_____

_____

_____

_____

_____

_____

_____

_____

11. God gets angry

Psalm 7:11 God judgeth the righteous, and God is angry [with the wicked] every day.
Mark 3:4-5

In humans, anger is a basically a strong feeling of displeasure or hostility; an emotional state that may range in intensity from mild irritation to intense fury and rage. Anger has physical effects including raising the heart rate and blood pressure and the levels of adrenaline and noradrenalin. We must manage our anger or more importantly the actions that are caused by anger.

 In Mark 3:4-5, Jesus is confronted about healing on the Sabbath. Jesus sees a man in need; a man with a withered hand; a man hurting; a man wanting to be healed. Yet, the people who know the law are so caught up in the law that they forget about grace, mercy, and compassion. Because their hearts were so hard, Jesus became angry. Mark 3:5 says "And when he had looked round about on them with anger, being grieved for the hardness of their hearts". Jesus converted his anger into healing. The man's hand was restored and made whole.

The bible records that God does get angry at wicked people and God judges the righteous. Therefore if you are righteous and some wicked person does something evil against you, know that God is indeed taking note of them and may even get angry at them. Also know that just like Jesus healed out of anger, God may bless the righteous who have been oppressed or transgressed out of anger. Micah 7:18 reminds us that (God) "retaineth not his anger for ever, because he delighteth [in] mercy." Have a Great Day!

Prayer
O God, thank you for provision and your protection. If I have angered you, O God, have mercy upon me. Forgive me of my sins. In Jesus' Name, Amen.

Personal Reflections

Date: _____

Thoughts:_____

_____

_____

_____

This Day's Objective:_____

_____

_____

_____

_____

_____

12. Remembering the Blood

Exodus 12:23-24 For the LORD will pass through to smite the Egyptians; and when he seeth the blood upon the lintel, and on the two side posts, the LORD will pass over the door, and will not suffer the destroyer to come in unto your houses to smite [you]. And ye shall observe this thing for an ordinance to thee and to thy sons for ever.

The Jewish people to this day remember how God protected them by the power the blood of a lamb. The blood provided the distinction for protection. To the Jewish People, remembrance of the Passover is mandated forever so that generations upon generations will know how God delivered the Jewish people from slavery to freedom.

Today, all people can be covered under the protection of the blood of the Holy lamb, which is Jesus Christ. (1 Peter 1:18-19) Forasmuch as ye know that ye were not redeemed with corruptible things, [as] silver and gold, from your vain conversation [received] by tradition from your fathers; But with the precious blood of Christ, as of a lamb without blemish and without spot:(1 Corinthians 11:23-26)   Therefore Christians around the world remember the sacrifice that Jesus made for the remission of our sins. The Lord Jesus the [same] night in which he was betrayed took bread: And when he had given thanks, he brake [it], and said, Take, eat: this is my body, which is broken for you: this do in remembrance of me. After the same manner also [he took] the cup, when he had supped, saying, This cup is the new testament in my blood: this do ye, as oft as ye drink [it], in remembrance of me. For as often as ye eat this bread, and drink this cup, ye do shew the Lord's death till he come. For God so loved the world that He gave his only begotten son that whosever believeth in Him should not perish but have everlasting life. (John 3:16)

 Have a Great day!

Prayer

O God of Ages Past, Hallowed be thy name. Thank you for your mercy and grace. Thank you for your son, Jesus Christ, who died for the remission of my sins. I confess my sins to you God that I may be

forgiven. Thank you for my Lord and Savior, Jesus
Christ. In the name of Jesus.

Personal Reflections

Date: _____

Thoughts:_____

_____

_____

_____

_____

_____

This Day's Objective:_____

_____

_____

_____

_____

_____

13. Peace of Mind

Philemon 4:8-9 Finally, brethren, whatsoever things are true, whatsoever things [are] honest, whatsoever things [are] just, whatsoever things [are] pure, whatsoever things [are] lovely, whatsoever things [are] of good report; if [there be] any virtue, and if [there be] any praise, think on these things. Those things, which ye have both learned, and received, and heard, and seen in me, do: and the God of peace shall be with you.

One week day evening as the children came in the house from a day of school, Mrs. Brown waved a greeting at the children as she continued stirring her pot of collard greens with her right hand while holding the telephone to her ear with the other hand. "Now Ruthie, if Janie Mae says one more thing about me I'm gonna give her a piece of my mind! Who do she think she is? Yeah, chile! I heard she's about to lose her car anyway. She needs to tend to her business and keep that car rather than trying to mind my business!"

Everyone wants peace of mind, so we don't always need to give a piece of it away. Much of that depends on how we utilize our minds. We determine what we read, what we watch on television, what kind of movies we watch, what kind of telephone conversations we participate in, what kind of comments come out our mouth, and basically whether we choose to see a glass half full or half empty. God grants peace to those who diligently seek him. We seek Him by thinking on good things, meditating on scripture, finding good in situations, viewing the world with honest lenses, and most importantly looking to the hills from whence cometh our help. Our help comes from the Lord who made heaven and earth. If you want peace of mind, watch what you think about and change it by the choices you make. Have a Great Day!

Prayer

O God, grant me peace of mind. In Jesus Name. Amen.

Personal Reflections

Date: _____

Thoughts:_____

_____

_____

_____

This Day's Objective:_____

_____

_____

_____

_____

14. Down but Not Out

2 Corinthians 4:8-9,14 [We are] troubled on every side, yet not distressed; [we are] perplexed, but not in despair; Persecuted, but not forsaken; cast down, but not destroyed; Knowing that he which raised up the Lord Jesus shall raise up us also by Jesus, and shall present [us] with you. For which cause we faint not; but though our outward man perish, yet the inward [man] is renewed day by day.

Hurricanes, Tsunami's, and even earthquakes are common occurrences based on news casts. Strangers and even family members killing other family members are reported in news programs, papers, and media all across the world. Reports of voter right's infringement, social unrest, failing social security, and dishonest politicians and public leaders seem to plague our minds. Yet, as believers of Jesus Christ with faith in God, we are not distressed or despair. As we still find reason to smile, to laugh, and rejoice in the Lord because we know that the same God who has power and authority to raise Jesus from the dead, has the power to handle the many situations that come up in our life. "Our hope is built on nothing less than Jesus blood and his righteousness" as quoted from the popular hymn, "My Hope is Built". We have hope because of Immanuel, "God with us". God is with you as you move through your day. At your office, in your car, in your meeting, in the bathroom, along the highway, or on the bus, have a talk with him or just thank him for being there.

Have a great day!

Prayer

O God,
Even though trials come may way, I trust in You to
see me through those situations. God, make the
crooked places straight and rough places smooth.
Thank you for being with me. In the name of Jesus,
Amen.

Personal Reflections

Date: _____

Thoughts:_____

_____

_____

_____

_____

This Day's Objective:_____

_____

_____

_____

_____

_____

15. Greatness in Africa

Nahum 3:9-10 Ethiopia and Egypt [were] her strength, and [it was] infinite; Put and Lubim were thy helpers.

When asked "where are you from", most people say something like "I'm from Alabama". As a people, people of African descent have heritage which goes beyond Alabama. Nineveh was a great city around 700 BC in ancient Assyria which is located in the present day area of Iraq and Mosul located near the Tigris River. The city was great because of its location and role in commercial routes of that day. Nineveh is also famous due to the prophet Jonah who was swallowed by the big fish and was released to spread the word of the Lord to the people. In the book of Nahum which is a recording of prophesies by Nahum the Elkoshite which denotes the village of Elkosh in Gallilee. The prophet Nahum is speaking to the people of Nineveh and warns that even though Nineveh has a relationship with the "great" nations of Egypt and Ethiopia; Nineveh has to give in account for its transgressions against God. It's not the first indication that there is a biblical account of greatness in Africa, but it is definitely an explicit citation. For people of color, it is a historical account to connect them with a heritage beyond 400 years of slavery in the United States, the Caribbean, Europe, and even on the Continent of Africa. There was strength and greatness in Africa and there were even beautiful people in Africa. Solomon's beautiful lady love of his life refers to herself as "black, but comely (beautiful)" (Song of Songs 1:5) according to the 1611 King James translation which occurred during the period of

African slavery. However today, most biblical scholars translate this phrase as "black and beautiful". For people of color, here is a historical and biblical account of strength and beauty in people of color that is over 2,000 years old. What's even greater is the Genesis 1:26 account which says "And God said, Let us make man in our image, after our likeness." All humankind is created in the image of God. Today, let's be thankful for our loving creator who made each of us like we are.

Have a Great Day!

Prayer

O God, thank you for all humanity. Thank you for persons of African descent, European descent, Asian descent, and basically all your children. In Jesus' Name, Amen.

Personal Reflections

Date: _____

Thoughts:_____

_____

_____

_____

_____

_____

_____

This Day's Objective:_____

_____

_____

_____

_____

_____

_____

16. Serving God in the Wilderness

Exodus 7:16 And thou shalt say unto him, The LORD God of the Hebrews hath sent me unto thee, saying, Let my people go, that they may serve me in the wilderness: and, behold, hitherto thou wouldest not hear.

A young man told a story of a funeral that he was trying to attend. He left home headed toward this funeral which was several miles away so he traveled in his car at speeds in excess of 85 miles per hour. He came upon a terrible storm with strong winds, down pouring rains, lightening, and thunder. As he entered the storm he was forced to slow down to 70, but he kept moving. The storm became more intense as he moved along the highway. He was forced to slow down to 60 then 50. He noticed hail began to fall as the winds blew harder. Cars began to slow down along side him as the rain became more intense. He slowed down to 35 then to 25. Other cars pulled over and parked on the side of the highway, yet he kept moving. Forced to slow down even more because of poor visibility, he was moving at 15 miles an hour. More cars pulled over and parked. After about an hour driving, the rain the stopped and the clouds cleared. The sun shone brightly as the clear blue skies was decorated with birds flying through the air. The young man was just awed at the beauty around him because he remembered the storm he had just left. Then he remembered all the people parked on the side of the road. These people were still in the storm.

God had promised Abraham greatness and that all his children would be blessed. Before the children of Israel would see the land promised to them, God let them know that they would have to serve Him in the wilderness. When you have tough times, it is not the time to stop serving or praising God. Even if you have to slow down, don't stop. "Ye though I walk through the valley of the shadow of death, I will fear no evil. Thy rod and thy staff they comfort me...surely goodness and mercy shall follow me all the days of my life and I will dwell in the house of the Lord forever."(Psalm 23) Serve God in and out of season, in and out of your job, in and out of your church, in and out of your home, and in and out of where ever you are!

 Have a great day!

Personal Reflections

Date: _____

Thoughts:_____

_____

_____

_____

_____

_____

_____

This Day's Objective:_____

_____

_____

_____

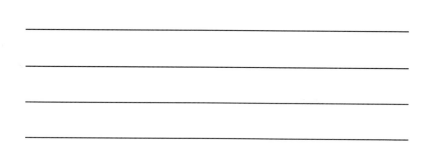

17. Telling the next generation

Psalm 78:3-4 Things we have heard and known, that our ancestors have told us. We will not hide them from their children; we will tell to the coming generation the glorious deeds of the Lord, and his might and wonders that He has done.

Sir Isaac Newton realized that objects fall toward the earth and noted it as gravity. From his discovery, other thinkers found certain truths regarding how objects move toward the earth. Leonardo DaVinci is another who made observations about how things work and noted it. There are countless numbers of people throughout history who have learned certain truths in their lives and have passed those truths onto future generations. Just as we celebrate the discovery of the properties of electricity, we should celebrate how God has worked in the lives of humankind. Indigenous African culture holds in high esteem ancestors. The relationship of ancestors to the all powerful deity is told and retold to generations. This habit of telling and retelling the story of the people is embedded deep within African culture.

Somewhere along the line, many African descendents felt that their story was not important and stopped telling the story. Now, many African descendents are seeking identity in a world that tends to try to give you an identity. Television ads and commercials try to tell society how to look, walk, talk, dress, smell, and even eat. Some forms of television will even try to tell you what you should think about God, but it is the role of this generation to pass on the story of how God has moved in their lives. They should tell "the glorious deeds of the Lord, and his might and wonders that He has done." One of the most beautiful things to remember is your parent or grandparent praying or singing the wondrous love of Jesus. Now, tell it.

Have a great day!

Prayer

O God, thank you for my heritage. Help me to remember to continue to tell the story of my heritage and how you have blessed us and will continue to be with us in the future. In Jesus' Name.

Personal Reflections

Date: _____

Thoughts:_____

_____

_____

_____

_____

_____

This Day's Objective:_____

_____

_____

_____

_____

_____

18. Giving God your heart

Luke 18:20-22 Thou knowest the commandments, Do not commit adultery, Do not kill, Do not steal, Do not bear false witness, Honour thy father and thy mother. And he said, All these have I kept from my youth up. Now when Jesus heard these things, he said unto him, Yet lackest thou one thing: sell all that thou hast, and distribute unto the poor, and thou shalt have treasure in heaven: and come, follow me.

Many people want to find the magic solution for all their problems or situations. The rationale is that if I work, I will be rich; if I obey the laws, I won't have any dealings with the law; if I go to church, I will never have issues; if I obey the ten commandments, I am going to heaven. Of course, we recognize that many people still struggle with keeping the Ten Commandments. Jesus taught this lesson to the man who had kept the commandments according to the law. The man thought he had done enough to enter the kingdom of heaven, but Jesus let him know that he was still lacking something. He lacked the heart or temperament of God. The man lacked compassion because he was unwilling to give up what he had to give to the poor and follow Christ.   Following Christ is not always the easy road. For centuries many Christians were persecuted, beaten, and even killed. What cost would you pay to follow Christ? Would you love your enemy, have compassion on a known felon, feed a hungry family, or clothe a known crack addict? (1 John 4:20) If a man say, I love God, and hateth his brother, he is a liar: for he that loveth not his brother whom he hath seen, how can he love God whom he hath not seen?

Have a great day!

Prayer

O God, help me to be devoted to you. I offer my heart to you and rededicate my life you. Let me be pleasing in your sight. In Jesus' Name.

Personal Reflections

Date: _____

Thoughts:_____

_____

_____

_____

_____

_____

_____

This Day's Objective:_____

_____

_____

_____

_____

_____

_____

19. Power of Love

Genesis: 29:20 And Jacob served seven years for Rachel; and they seemed unto him [but] a few days, for the love he had to her.

Stephanie Mills, a very talented rhythm and blues singer, sang a song entitled "The Power of Love". The lyrics are "I was a victim of my foolish thinking; Carelessly I've risked my love and my life; There's no self-pity, I admit I obliged; Overpowered by love I pretended to be blind; Faith has survived all the doubts I've summoned my heart has stood all the failure and loss; Helpless I cannot further be driven; I've learned to respect the power of love".   Love is not a new thing. In fact, it is one of the most sought after emotions by all humankind. This kind of love mentioned in this song runs deep and many times causes people to do things that they normally would not do.

Jacob served seven years for Rachel due to the love he had for her. He loved her so much that he was willing to work over 21 years to gain her hand in marriage.   Jacob eventually gained Rachel's hand in marriage but at great costs, yet he loved her until death. Samson on the other hand loved someone who deceived him. (Judges 16:4) After he had fallen victim to lies and deception, he was blinded and had to turn to God to redeem himself. (Judges 6:34). How love makes people act is an area that is biblically dealt with, dealt with in many popular songs, story lines, shows, movies, but seldom dealt with in the church. To help us respond to this powerful emotion called love, God leaves us some advice found in Malachi 3:16-18. Those that fear God and keep His commandments shall be able to discern between righteous and wicked; between those who serve God and those who don't serve God. It still may not give you the answer to your love situation. So as we deal with this power of love, one approach is to pray the psalmist prayer (119:125): I [am] thy servant; give me understanding, that I may know thy testimonies. If you have found a love, nourish it in the ways of God that it may grow and be blessed. If it's not that kind of love, don't pretend that is. You can't make an apple out of an orange. Be patient. Ecclesiastes 3:11 "To every [thing there is] a season, and a time to every purpose under the heaven:"

Have a great day!

Prayer

O God, Thank you for the ability to love. Thank you for you love that you continue to give us. Lead me and guide me to be a good steward of love. In Jesus' Name. Amen.

Personal Reflections

Date: _____

Thoughts:_____

_____

_____

_____

_____

_____

_____

This Day's Objective:_____

_____

_____

_____

_____

_____

_____

_____

20. Liberty

Jeremiah 34:17 Therefore thus saith the LORD;
Ye have not hearkened unto me, in proclaiming
liberty, every one to his brother, and every man to
his neighbour: behold, I proclaim a liberty for you,
saith the LORD, to the sword, to the pestilence,
and to the famine; and I will make you to be
removed into all the kingdoms of the earth.

As early as 1615, persons like John Ogilvie, a Jesuit, was watched by the government, tried, sentenced to death, and even mutilated after death because of his religious beliefs.   Thousands of Protestants and Catholics escaped Europe to North America to seek freedom of expression, religion, press, and much more.

 While Europeans sought freedoms by escaping to Colonies in North America, twenty Africans are recorded as being brought by a Dutch man of war and sold to the English colony of Jamestown, Virginia in 1619 as indentured servants. By 1640, Virginia courts had sentenced at least one black servant to slavery. Then in 1661, slavery was referenced in Virginia law as a part of the very fabric of of the governing colonies and then becoming official in 1705 as part of the Slave Code which sealed slavery as a way of life for African Americans, even though some colonies like Rhode Island banned slavery in 1774.

The United States celebrates its independence from Great Britain as marked by the July 4, 1776 date in which the Declaration of Independence was adopted by the Continental Congress of the thirteen original colonies. While this new nation celebrated its liberty, it denied liberty to some of its hardest working and productive citizens, the African Americans. While President Abraham Lincoln attempted to emancipate the slaves on January 1, 1863 which later cost him his life, slavery in the United States did not cease until as late as June 19, 1865 . In 1867, federal law was enacted to prohibit the next step of bondage in the United States began with debt bondage or peonage. Undoubtedly, many argue that economic liberty is still an issue for the African American people in the new millennium. Even in the year 2006, no official apology has been offered to the African American people for the damage and effects that slavery has inflicted on them as a people.

As a good barometer, children of God must look to God in understanding what liberty is all about and secondly how to implement true liberty. Fortunately, African American people and other people of God throughout time and throughout the world have turned to God for freedom and liberty. (John 8:36 If the Son therefore shall make you free, ye shall be free indeed.) Let's be thankful for a God of mercy, grace, and liberty.

 Have a Great Day!

Prayer

O Gracious God, Thank you for liberating spirit. Help us to be good stewards of your freedom and our responsibility to extend freedom to all humankind.

Help us to be in your divine will as we celebrate your freedom. In Jesus' Name. Amen.

Personal Reflections

Date: _____

Thoughts:_____

_____

_____

_____

_____

_____

_____

This Day's Objective:_____

_____

_____

_____

_____

_____

_____

21. Forgiveness

Matthew 18:21-22 Then came Peter to him, and said, Lord, how oft shall my brother sin against me, and I forgive him? till seven times? Jesus saith unto him, I say not unto thee, Until seven times: but, Until seventy times seven.

Little Johnny was told by his father not ride his bicycle in the street. Little Johnny deduced that riding the bicycle in the yard was not enough so he rode the bicycle in the street because no one was looking and there were no cars seen moving on the street. Little Johnny did not see his father watching him through an upstairs window.   Minutes later little Johnny heard his father calling him. He went to see what his father wanted. His father said "Johnny, you disobeyed me. Because you disobeyed me, you may not ride the bicycle any more this week. Because I love you, I will forgive you and next week you may ride the bicycle. If you ride in the street, you may get hurt and I don't want you to get hurt, so I will sell your bicycle."

All of us want to be forgiven for things we do that we know we shouldn't do. Sometimes we unknowingly do things that require forgiveness as well.   When Christ taught us to pray, forgiveness was part of the formula for prayer: "...forgive us our trespasses as we forgive those who trespass against us..."   Not forgiving someone keeps a part of our own being bound and captive. To experience freedom, we must free others by forgiving them.

Have a Great Day!

Prayer

O God, help me to be more forgiving to those who trespass against me. Forgive me of my trespasses. In Jesus' Name. Amen

Personal Reflections

Date: _____

Thoughts:_____

_____

_____

_____

_____

This Day's Objective:_____

_____

_____

_____

_____

_____

22. Making Parents Proud

3 John 1:4 I have no greater joy than to hear that my children walk in truth.

Beginning at birth, children develop and build on what they experience in the world. They look to parents, guardians, and other adults for role models. One of the basic skills learned is speech. As children develop their ability to speak, they soak up the words used in the household, on television, on the radio, and even on video games. If they hear profanity, they tend to articulate profanity well. If they are forbidden to lie, they tend to be as truthful as they can be, of course there are exceptions. As they get older, many children seek to find approval and affirmation by the role models in their life.

What makes parents, guardians, and other nurturers proud is to see the child grow into maturity and make good decisions on their own. Shirley Caesar echoed the sentiment in her song "Hold My Mule". An old man was forbidden from expression of his joy at the local church because it distracted the other church members and it was considered unacceptable behavior by the other church members. The deacons of the church visited the man while he was plowing his field to talk to him about his behavior. He replied to them that God had blessed him with the land in which they were standing. God had also blessed him to not have to go get any of his children out of jail and all his children were living. For that reason he was giving God glory, honor, and praise for protecting and keeping his children. One of the greatest joys of parents is to see their children walk in truth.

58

Many adults take pride in seeing future generations take the mantle of leadership, responsibility, and community. Of course to get the children to this level, adults must train the child in the way he should go. When the child is old, he will not depart. (Proverbs 22:6) As an adult, I understand why my grandmother would have this look of deep pity before she spanked me for doing something that I should not have done. She would always say "This hurts me to have to spank you, but you were wrong." She would explain why she was giving me the spanking. It would be the most memorable spanking. When you do well, parents, grandparents, and other care givers and nurturers take pride in seeing you do well. The same applies to future generations.

Have a great day!

Prayer

O God,

Thank you for the role models in my life who tried to train me to live a good life. Help me to be a good role model for future generations. Help me to give sound guidance pleasing in your sight to growing future adults. In Jesus' Name. Amen.

Personal Reflections

Date: _____

Thoughts:_____

_____

_____

_____

_____

_____

_____

This Day's Objective:_____

_____

_____

_____

_____

_____

_____

23. Too Proud

James 4:6 But he giveth more grace. Wherefore he saith, God resisteth the proud, but giveth grace unto the humble.

Ever since moving into the subdivision, Mr. Smith had the best kept lawn in the neighborhood. Finely pruned hedges, beautiful, budding daffodils, lilacs, gardenias, and roses painted a beautiful portrait of color for all to see each day as they pass Mr. Smith's house. For over 30 years, Mr. Smith prided himself in having a beautiful yard and he did all the work himself. As Mr. Smith approached 70, he realized that he could not stay in the sun as long or even stoop as long to pull weeds out his flower garden. The beautiful yard began to become over grown with weeds and the hedges lost their precise form. Mr. Smith, however, being the proud man that he was, Mr. Smith refused to ask for help or even attempt to hire help.

Mrs. Smith realized that her husband needed some help and mentioned it to her next door neighbor, Mrs. Jones. Mrs. Jones said that her son had always admired Mr. Smith and the work that he did in his yard. Mrs. Jones' son said that he longed for the opportunity to work beside Mr. Smith, but it seemed that Mr. Smith would never allow it. Both ladies, seeing a common need, realized that Mrs. Jones' son could work with Mr. Smith and return the beauty that the yard had possessed for so many years. Mrs. Smith asked the young man to help her and he was so excited that he immediately ran over to begin work on the hedges. After hearing noise outside his window, Mr. Smith went to the front door to see what caused the noise. Then Mrs. Smith chimed in "It's time to let someone help us. That young man may need some advice though. Would you go out and tell him about the shortcuts?" Realizing that the young man may need him, Mr. Smith smiled and went outside to speak to the young man. Once again, the Smith yard was beautiful living portrait of greenery and flowers.

Being too proud can often cause us to experience hardship and unnecessary labor that can be avoided only if we humble ourselves and simply ask for help. Being afraid to say "I don't know" or "I can't do this by myself" can be a life disenabling characteristic. God does want us to be all that we are created to be and do all that we are created to do, but pride can make us forget that we are sharing this world with many people with many gifts and graces. (Ecclesiastes 4:9-10) "Two [are] better than one; because they have a good reward for their labour. For if they fall, the one will lift up his fellow: but woe to him [that is] alone when he falleth; for [he hath] not another to help him up."

Have a great day!

Prayer

God, Help me to be humble. Don't let me my foolish pride disenable me or stop me from being all that you have created me. Put the right people and opportunities in my path. Be a light in my path so that

I may grow into what you desire me to be. In Jesus' Name.

Personal Reflections

Date: _____

Thoughts:_____

_____

_____

_____

_____

_____

This Day's Objective:_____
                                        .

_____

_____

_____

_____

_____

_____

24. Participating in Worship

Nehemiah 8:4-8 And Ezra the scribe stood upon a pulpit of wood, which they had made for the purpose; and beside him stood Mattithiah, and Shema, and Anaiah, and Urijah, and Hilkiah, and Maaseiah, on his right hand; and on his left hand, Pedaiah, and Mishael, and Malchiah, and Hashum, and Hashbadana, Zechariah, [and] Meshullam. And Ezra opened the book in the sight of all the people; (for he was above all the people;) and when he opened it, all the people stood up: And Ezra blessed the LORD, the great God. And all the people answered, Amen, Amen, with lifting up their hands: and they bowed their heads, and worshipped the LORD with [their] faces to the ground. Also Jeshua, and Bani, and Sherebiah, Jamin, Akkub, Shabbethai, Hodijah, Maaseiah, Kelita, Azariah, Jozabad, Hanan, Pelaiah, and the Levites, caused the people to understand the law: and the people [stood] in their place. So they read in the book in the law of God distinctly, and gave the sense, and caused [them] to understand the reading.

As we take time to spend reading our daily scriptures and worshiping in our sanctuaries around the world, make sure we are not simply going through the motions or let worship become some mundane task, but be intentional and purposeful. "Going to church" because mother or father said it is good, is not good enough any more. We must move to getting an understanding. Those who lead in worship must help the people understand. Those who attend must look for ways to understand. Ezra allowed the people to share in his reading by standing up. The people responded to him by saying "Amen" and "lifting their hands". Their participation helped them reach an understanding. When you go to church, it is your time to participate so you can get an understanding. Psalm 47:7 "For God [is] the King of all the earth: sing ye praises with understanding."

Have a Great Day!

Prayer

O God, help me to worship you in spirit in truth. Send you Holy Spirit to lead me and guide me so that I may please you. Let me be an instrument of praise. Allow understanding to take place so that I may grow into all that you would have me to be. In Jesus' name. Amen.

Personal Reflections

Date: _____

Thoughts:_____

_____

_____

_____

_____

_____

_____

This Day's Objective:_____

_____

_____

_____

_____

_____

_____

25. God is Faithful to His Promises

Hebrew 6:12-15 That ye be not slothful, but followers of them who through faith and patience inherit the promises. For when God made promise to Abraham, because he could swear by no greater, he sware by himself, Saying, Surely blessing I will bless thee, and multiplying I will multiply thee. And so, after he had patiently endured, he obtained the promise.

Get up every morning, take a shower, brush your teeth, put on clothes, and turn the news on the television or radio. Go wake up the kids, fix breakfast for the kids, comb the girls hair, take out clothes for youngest child to wear, and put all your papers in your brief case to take to work. Drop off the kids at the babysitter, school, and then go to work. The laundry lists of things to do every day can seem mundane and even overwhelming some days, but be not weary in well doing. (2 Thessalonians 3:13) God made a promise to Abraham that he would bless him and all his children. Through Abraham we receive Jesus, God's gift to the world, that whosoever believes in Him should not perish but everlasting life. God did not promise us that we would not have to work or have to get up every morning. However God did not leave us without wise counsel: Exodus 23:12 "Six days thou shalt do thy work, and on the seventh day thou shalt rest: that thine ox and thine ass may rest, and the son of thy handmaid, and the stranger, may be refreshed." Therefore we have no reason to be slothful, but we should diligently be followers of them that inherit the promises, a follower of Christ in all that we do. Celebrate having the mind to get up in the morning, the strength to face the day's challenges and victories, and the humbleness to know that you didn't do it alone, but it was God who helped you do it.

Have a Great Day!

Prayer

O God, Thank you for work to do. Be with me through this day. Give me the daily bread to make it through

*this day with success. At the end of this week, help
me rest. In Jesus' Name. Amen.*

Personal Reflections

Date: _____

Thoughts:_____

_____

_____

_____

_____

_____

This Day's Objective:_____

_____

_____

_____

_____

_____

26. Prayer for Peace

Philippians 4:6-7 Be careful for nothing; but in every thing by prayer and supplication with thanksgiving let your requests be made known unto God. And the peace of God, which passeth all understanding, shall keep your hearts and minds through Christ Jesus.

Humans have a power and authority to do many things such as operate motor vehicles, create exquisite gourmet meals, and even talk to each other using cellular telephones. While it seems that humans have control over these operations, God creates the milk, vegetable, meat, and grain to make the meals. God also creates minerals and other natural resources that are used to build the car and cellular telephone. God even gives humankind the knowledge to pull all the pieces together to create and use. Therefore, Paul, realizing the limitedness of humans in the grand scheme of things, says "Be careful for nothing." For all that God does that we know and all that we don't know, we should thank God. Knowing that we can talk to God in prayer, we should have peace because we know we are never alone. The hymn writer says "I come to the garden alone while the dew is still on the roses..." yet he "Walks with me and talks with me and tells me I am His own." Because we can talk to God any time, any where about any thing, it will bring peace which passeth all understanding in our hearts and minds. If you really want peace, talk to God in prayer. Have some peace today as you talk to God. Have a great day!!

Prayer

O God, thank you for all things. I need you present in my life today. Give me peace to face the challenges of this day. In Jesus' Name. Amen.

Personal Reflections

Date: _____

Thoughts:_____

_____

_____

_____

_____

This Day's Objective:_____

_____

_____

_____

_____

_____

27. One of the Few

Luke 10:2 Therefore said he unto them, The harvest truly [is] great, but the labourers [are] few: pray ye therefore the Lord of the harvest, that he would send forth labourers into his harvest.

An iranian-American philanthropist named Pierre Omidyar graduated from Tufts University with a computer science degree and joined Claris, an Apple affiliate. While at the age of 28, there were millions of internet users, but he sat down and wrote the code to what became the Ebay auction site. Today, Omidyar's stock in the Ebay enterprise is worth around $8 billion. How is it that in the midst of so many, only a few step out to be leaders in any particular area? Jesus was speaking to his disciples in this Luke 10:2 verse. He had just sent seventy who would go out two by two to prepare the way for him. One reason is that everyone will not stick to what needs to be done in order to produce the desired results. Jesus says in Luke 9:62 that "No man, having put his hand to the plough, and looking back, is fit for the kingdom of God." There is much to gain because the harvest is still great, but the laborer or number of people willing to grab the plough and press forward are few. There are some historical laborers that have made significant gains by sticking to the plough such as Mary McCloud Bethune who started Bethune-Cookman College and even George Washington Carver who sought and found hundreds of uses for the peanut. Oseola McCarty, a resident of Hattiesburg, Mississippi, showed what stick-to-it-ness can do." Miss McCarty was the town's washer woman who said that "People didn't think there was money in washing, but there was." This woman who never owned a car or seldom used an air conditioner gave $150,000 to the University of Southern Mississippi, the largest gift ever by a Black to a Mississippi university. The money establishes an endowed scholarship fund, with priority given to needy Black students. Will you be one of the few?

Have a great day!

Prayer

O God, help me to see beyond my circumstance to the place where you desire me to be. Order my steps in your word; be a light unto my path; and lead me to that place. Guide me and keep all along the way. In Jesus' Name. Amen.

Personal Reflections

Date: _____

Thoughts:_____

_____

_____

_____

_____

_____

This Day's Objective:_____

_____

_____

_____

_____

_____

_____

_____

28. God's Voice

Deuteronomy 28:1-2 And it shall come to pass, if thou shalt hearken diligently unto the voice of the LORD thy God, to observe [and] to do all his commandments which I command thee this day, that the LORD thy God will set thee on high above all nations of the earth: And all these blessings shall come on thee, and overtake thee, if thou shalt hearken unto the voice of the LORD thy God.

I once saw a t-shirt that said "Real Men Pray".   It was a simple yet profound statement.   Katherine J. Emerick, a psychologist quoted by "U.S. News and World Report" says "In my twenty-three years as a psychologist, I have learned that, above all, my clients need to be heard, understood, and responded to by their therapist. I believe in dialogue as a healing." According to Emerick, being heard and getting a response is a formidable part of the healing process. Generically, praying is our conversation with God. We can utter words through our mouths to God, but people unable to speak can still pray.   So, prayer becomes more than the utterance of the words. It is a time where we lift up our spirit to commune with the Spirit of God. It is a time when we intentionally express our wishes and desires to the God of the most high. As we pray, we also look for an answer. Like the psychologist Emerick, I believe there are healing and blessings in listening for and hearing the voice of God.   The voice may say no, yes, and even wait. Biblical writers many times used the word listen or hearing synonymously with doing something directly related to what is heard. In other words, if you heard the voice of God say love your neighbor, you will love your neighbor. If you really hear the voice of God, you will obey his commandments. The promise is "that the LORD thy God will set thee on high above all nations of the earth: And all these blessings shall come on thee, and overtake thee."   While you pray any time and any where, listen for voice of God. Sometimes you may not understand what you hear, but those are the times to pray for understanding and discernment. (Job 37:5) "God thundereth marvellously with his voice; great things doeth he, which we cannot comprehend."   We have a promise in 2 Chronicles 7:14 "If my people, which are called by my name, shall humble themselves, and pray, and seek my face, and turn from their wicked ways; then will I hear from heaven, and will forgive their sin, and will heal their land." Whatever it is, take it to God in prayer and listen for the voice of God to answer.

HAVE A GREAT DAY!

Prayer

God, help me to hear your voice. I'm seeking answers to life's difficult questions. Give me peace as I wait and listen for the answer. In Jesus' Name. Amen

Personal Reflections

Date: _____

Thoughts:_____

_____

_____

_____

_____

_____

This Day's Objective:_____

_____

_____

_____

_____

_____

_____

29. Believing in Prayer

Mark 11:24 Therefore I say unto you, What things soever ye desire, when ye pray, believe that ye receive [them], and ye shall have [them].

A certain man faced eviction from his home and very little to provide for himself. He did have a job but the job was not paying the amount of wages that he was accustomed.   He also had a gift for singing.   He felt that God had blessed him with a voice to bless others in the church, but he could not find a church that he felt comfortable singing.   He prayed that God would meet his financial needs and then he would offer his gift of singing in return. Months passed and he never was evicted from his home while he had food to eat, clothes to wear, and transportation to get around. He asked God when will God going to bless him abundantly. The previous verse of Markan chapter addresses this issue to a degree: "For verily I say unto you, That whosoever shall say unto this mountain, Be thou removed, and be thou cast into the sea; and shall not doubt in his heart, but shall believe that those things which he saith shall come to pass; he shall have whatsoever he saith." What this man had been asking God to do was to bless him if he offered his voice for service to the church. He never offered his voice, yet God did hear his prayer and allowed him to keep his home. God even provided for his daily means of survival. Where he was looking for abundance in money, God blessed him with an opportunity to let his faith grow and his walk with God to become closer and more personal. Where he was looking for a high paying job, God allowed him to become witness to people on his job and other places he went when he had not been able to share the goodness of being a child of God before. He stated that now he had to recognize that God was the author and finisher of his faith. As he came upon this realization, one of the people he witnessed to arranged for him to interview for a new job which paid more money. He interviewed and is now starting the new job. It may be that his mountain was moving all along but he was just to close to see how far it was moving. The ball is now in his court as it relates to the singing. God has been faithful to answering this young man's prayer, but will he be faithful to his service. God answers prayer to those who believe in their prayer. What are you praying for? In looking for the answer, you should look through open lenses.   The answer may have already come or is coming.

 Have a great day!

Prayer
O God, thank you for the ability to pray to you. Help me increase my faith in my prayer life.   In Jesus' Name. Amen.

Personal Reflections

Date: _____

Thoughts:_____

_____

_____

_____

_____

_____

This Day's Objective:_____

_____

_____

_____

_____

_____

_____

30. In the Midst of Mess

Psalm 138:7 Though I walk in the midst of trouble, thou wilt revive me: thou shalt stretch forth thine hand against the wrath of mine enemies, and thy right hand shall save me.

Mrs. Smith, a busy, professional woman in her own right, was raising three children while married to Mr. Smith. Mr. Smith, a very personable man, headed off to work every morning and returned in the evening. However, Mrs. Smith had begun to receive telephone calls concerning her husband being seen with a very attractive woman during the course of the day. Mrs. Smith reflected on the fact that her brother-in-law had just gone through a devastating divorce from a twenty year marriage due to adultery. Mrs. Smith found it increasingly difficult to ignore the calls and sought refuge in God. After praying and speaking with her husband, Mrs. Smith was reassured that her husband was faithful to her. Infidelity is always a very difficult and messy situation to be involved and it is adverse to the commandment which says "thou shall not commit adultery", but God can bring healing to any situation. With infidelity, primarily there is a breach of trust that is very difficult to regain. Breach of trust comes with other situations such as friends disclosing secrets, persons doing malicious things against them, or even sharing fictitious information. Those things are not of God because God is not the author of confusion. (Ephesians 6:12) " For we wrestle not against flesh and blood, but against principalities, against powers, against the rulers of the darkness of this world, against spiritual wickedness in high [places]." God will revive, protect, lead, and guide in the midst of any situation. As believers, we must keep the faith and seek guidance from God. The psalmist found a way to deal with mess in Psalm 119:133 when he said, "Order my steps in thy word: and let not any iniquity have dominion over me." In the midst of mess, "let Jesus lead you all the way from earth to heaven."

Have a great day!

Prayer

O God, Though I walk in the midst of trouble, thou wilt revive me: thou shalt stretch forth thine hand against the wrath of mine enemies, and thy right hand shall save me. In Jesus' Name, Amen.

Personal Reflections

Date: _____

Thoughts:_____

_____

_____

_____

_____

_____

This Day's Objective:_____

_____

_____

_____

_____

_____

_____

_____

31. Hospitality

1 Peter 4:9 Use hospitality one to another without grudging.

Hospitality means "cordial reception: kindness in welcoming guests or strangers". The bible tells us in Hebrew 13:2 to "Be not forgetful to entertain strangers: for thereby some have entertained angels unawares." There is something special and blessed about the ability to be hospitable. in the last thirty years, we have become very mobile around the world and communication media allow us to talk to one another via PDA, cellular phone, internet, and many other means. Yet when we meet strangers, or even familiar people, so many of us are so apprehensive about our safety that we have difficulty showing hospitality.

In the southern part of the United States, when coming into a room with people in it, the standard greeting is "Good Morning" or "hello".   If it's in Spanish, the greeting is "Hola"; In Japanese, it's "Konichiwa"; in Swahili, it's "Jambo"; in Chinese, it's "Ni hao"; in French, it's "Bonjour"; in Italian, it's "Buon giorno"; in Korean, it's "Annyong ha shimnikka"; in Polish, it's "Czesc"; in Russian, its "Zdravstvuite"; and in Arabic, it's "Al Salaam a' alaykum". Find a blessing in being hospitable. If you see someone you haven't seen today, just say "Hello".   Use hospitality without grudging and watch a blessing show up. Hello, Child of God!

Have a Super Day!

Prayer

O God, help met to be more hospitable to those persons that enter my space or I enter their space. In Jesus' Name. Amen.

Personal Reflections

Date: _____

Thoughts:_____

_____

_____

_____

_____

_____

This Day's Objective:_____

_____

_____

_____

_____

_____

32. Being a Citizen

Luke 2:4-5 And Joseph also went up from Galilee, out of the city of Nazareth, into Judaea, unto the city of David, which is called Bethlehem; (because he was of the house and lineage of David:) To be taxed with Mary his espoused wife, being great with child.

As children of God, some people get the idea that they don't need to participate in society or government. Government is subject to the authority of God whether it desires to be or not. Government is a system that helps people live together by providing for protection and other services to the people in exchange for the people supporting it. Ever since there have been governments, there have been good and bad leaders. Even the bible records good and bad leaders. Today, we have a President who is elected by the people who can have a conversation with another world leader using 'off-color' and profane language unknowingly while the world listened through microphones that were supposed to be turned off.   This leader can send troops into a sovereign nation citing "weapons of mass destruction" as the motive, yet never finding any mass weapons. Some people complain about having the leader, but they fail to participate in the voting process. Just as Joseph, even though his wife was pregnant with child, took his entire family with him to pay taxes to the government, each of us has a responsibility to participate in government where possible. In a great nation like the United States, we can participate through paying dreaded taxes and we can participate with our right to vote. As governors, representatives, judges, and even presidents seek election and re-election, we have to take up our mantle of citizenship and participate in the process. A representative from a well-known senator's office said that if his office receives five calls about any issue, it becomes a priority issue. Secondly, he said, when responding to calls, they typically look at the voting lists to see if the person participated in the voting process. I don't know if this is true or not, but it does give credence to responsibility in participating in the process. There are voting lists which capture who participates in what election and it is broken down by district, gender, and even ethnicity. Government leaders look at these lists when responding to issues. Even when Jesus was approaching Capernaum, he told Peter to go and look in the mouth of a fish in order that they may pay tribute or taxes to the King. (Matthew 17:24-27). Be a good citizen: Go Vote, Let your representative know your issues, and pay your taxes.

Have a great day!

Prayer

Sovereign God who has created all heaven and earth, help me to be a better steward of your creation and help me to participate in the political process by exercising my responsibilities as a citizen. In Jesus' Name. Amen.

Personal Reflections

Date: _____

Thoughts:_____

_____

_____

_____

_____

_____

This Day's Objective:_____

_____

_____

_____

_____

_____

_____

_____

33. Try the Spirit by the Spirit

1 John 4:1 Beloved, believe not every spirit, but try the spirits whether they are of God: because many false prophets are gone out into the world.

There is so much that comes at people in the modern world, yet religion is a cornerstone of human existence. Even the agnostic and atheist subscribe to some religious philosophy. Atheism is a disbelief in or denial of the existence of God or gods, which by its very nature has to acknowledge a God in order to disbelieve or deny a God. Agnosticism was defined by T.H. Huxley, the man who coined the term that means one should not profess to a belief in something that cannot be proven. However, all religion is based on perceived truths. In order to prove or disprove something, humankind must base their reasoning within confines of certain truths. Subsequently, there are evil people in the world who attempt to take advantage of religion in the life of humankind. God is greater than man's feeble attempt to explain and confine God within the scope of religion. Therefore as prophets, teachers, leaders, preachers, and whoever comes to you with proclamations, we are given wise counsel in 1 John 4 which is to try the spirit. God can speak to man, but God can send the Holy Spirit to give you understanding and the ability to bear witness to what is being said. Note in 2 Peter 1:20-21 that "Knowing this first, that no prophecy of the scripture is of any private interpretation."-- (In other words, it is not left to our own ability to give prophecy of scripture but only through the unction of the Holy Spirit.) -- "For the prophecy came not in old time by the will of man: but holy men of God spake [as they were] moved by the Holy Ghost." Job 32:8 "But [there is] a spirit in man: and the inspiration of the Almighty giveth them understanding." Continue to pray for understanding as you grow closer in your walk with God and watch God be faithful to His promises.

 Have a Great Day!

Prayer

God, Let your Holy Spirit abide in me to discern truth as it perceived, heard, felt, seen, or experienced that I my grow closer to you in my daily walk. In Jesus' Name. Amen.

Personal Reflections

Date: _____

Thoughts:_____

_____

_____

_____

_____

_____

This Day's Objective:_____

_____

_____

_____

_____

_____

_____

_____

34. Your Decision

Isaiah 6:8 Also I heard the voice of the Lord, saying, Whom shall I send, and who will go for us? Then said I, Here [am] I; send me.

There is a need for you to be something that meets a need. On July 19, 2006, the USA TODAY newspaper reported in an article, "In Tim Ryan's family, he is the addict" that "Addiction is endemic in American families. A USA TODAY/HBO nationwide poll of adults April 27-May 31 found that one in five said they had an immediate relative who at some point had been addicted to alcohol or drugs. That translates into roughly 40 million American adults with a spouse, parent, sibling or child battling addiction. And that doesn't count the millions of children living with an addicted parent." There are all types of addiction such as alcohol, drugs, sex, and many other forms. Ignoring them or not dealing with them hasn't made any of them go away. A decision has to be made who will spend their lives treating people with addictions and someone has to make the decision to get treated.

The same applies for many vocations such as accounting, medicine, the clergy, law, musical artists, and many more. Everyone has something that they can do in their lifetime. As a young lad, I used to hear adults say you need to go to school in order to get a good job. While that is true that education does affect one's ability to be placed in the workforce, the end is not to simply get a job. The key is making the decision to walk in your destiny. What is it that God desires you to do or to be?

Isaiah stopped to hear the word of the Lord saying that something needs to be done. Isaiah saw the pursuit of that vocation as his calling or the thing that fit him best so he answered "Here am I; send me". With the affect on the family by addiction and release of the USA Today article, someone, hopefully, is saying "Here am I. Send me. I will tackle the issue of addiction." Someone else might say, "Here am I. Send me. I will preach to sinners the liberating Gospel of Jesus Christ." Someone else might say, "Here am I. Send me. I will teach people how to

exercise and eat right so that they may be healthy."
Someone else might say, "Here am I. Send me. I will
open a business providing a service to my
community." What is it that God is speaking to you to
do? How long will it take you to hear it? Then, what is
your decision?

 Have a great day!

Prayer

*Dear Lord, with so many needs in the world, lead me
to the place and vocation that you desire me be.
Here I am, a willing vessel. Send me. I'll go. In
Jesus' Name. Amen*

Personal Reflections

Date: _____

Thoughts:_____

_____

_____

_____

_____

_____

This Day's Objective:_____

_____

_____

_____

_____

_____

_____

_____

35. Wash Day

Psalm 51:2 Wash me throughly from mine
iniquity, and cleanse me from my sin.

In the south as with many places around the country, there is a weekly ritual called Wash Day whereby all the dirty clothes within the house are gathered up and washed. I can remember one process was to go clean this huge black pot that could hold about 15-20 gallons of water. This pot was placed on some bricks as wood was strategically placed under the pot to burn. Once the fire was set, water was then toted (a country word for "carried") with buckets from the barrel which caught rain water from the corners of house during rain storms. Some type of cleaning solution such as soap powder but more commonly lye soap and bleach was put in the pot and the clothes were cooked, rinsed, and then wrung dry through two rolling pins that spun very closely together leaving only enough room to place the wet clothes between them. Only then were the clothes ready to shake and then hang on a clothesline to dry. There was nothing like the smell of fresh clean clothes. When Roman 3:23 tells us that all have sinned and come short of the glory of god, how can we be cleansed without some cleaning. Hebrew 12:27-29 tells us that those things shaken can be removed so the things unshaken can remain. Similarly, the kingdom of God can not be shaken or moved, so let us serve God "acceptably with reverence and godly fear: for our God is a consuming fire." Yes, the wages of sin is death and the gift of god is eternal life through Jesus Christ.(Romans 6:23).   We should praise God for the redeeming blood of Jesus which is expiation for our sins, but let us not forget that wash day may include some fire, some water, some cooking, some wringing, some rinsing, and even some drying. We do have a promise in 1 John 1:7 that "if we walk in the light, as he is in the light, we have fellowship one with another, and the blood of Jesus Christ his Son cleanseth us from all sin." Don't you just love wash day!!!

 Have a great day!

Prayer

O God, Forgive us our trespasses as we forgive those who trespass against us. Lead us not into temptation, but deliver us from evil. For thine is the Kingdom, the Power, and the Glory, Forever, Amen.

Personal Reflections

Date: _____

Thoughts:_____

_____

_____

_____

_____

_____

This Day's Objective:_____

_____

_____

_____

_____

_____

_____

_____

36. Some Battles You Do Fight

Joshua 10:25 And Joshua said unto them, Fear not, nor be dismayed, be strong and of good courage: for thus shall the LORD do to all your enemies against whom ye fight.

In life, there are battles you fight and there are some you don't fight. Unless you are killed, wars don't end with one fight so choose your battles carefully. If you fight, Joshua reminds us to be strong and of good courage. Hezekiah spoke the same sentiments in 1 Chronicles 32:7-8: "Be strong and courageous, be not afraid nor dismayed for the king of Assyria, nor for all the multitude that [is] with him: for [there be] more with us than with him: With him [is] an arm of flesh; but with us [is] the LORD our God to help us, and to fight our battles. And the people rested themselves upon the words of Hezekiah king of Judah."

While there is a word that says stand still and see the salvation of the Lord (Exodus 14:13), we must also realize that there are times when we must fight. There are ways to fight which are active and passive. The civil rights movement led by Rev. Dr. Martin Luther King, Jr. was effective because it was a passive aggressive movement seated in the righteousness of God and God's love for humanity which included boycotts, sit-ins, protests, and other methods in a non-violent way. At the same time, there was another movement which included active blatant aggressive violence by groups such as the black panthers. Both played a roll in causing change during that time.

Regardless of perceptions and analysis of the two group's credibility and effectiveness in the civil rights movement, the fact remains that no accomplishments were gained by doing nothing. Someone had to step and say this needs to be done and I am going to be the one who does it.

If you find yourself in a situation where you have to fight, it is always wise to pray for God's direction. Judges 9:38 records Gaal saying "...I pray now and fight with them" against Abimelech. Abimelech seemed to have won the battle, but we later find in verse 53 of the same chapter that "a certain woman cast a piece of a millstone upon Abimelech's head, and all to brake his skull." Abimelech, so embarrassed by the fact that woman had popped him in the head, called his armour bearer to slay him with a sword so the people would not know that a woman slew him with a rock.

As you go through your day, there may be some battles that you may have to fight, but don't fight alone or in malice, but with God's help on the side of justice. Fight on the side of the righteousness with prayer and supplication and watch God work in the midst of your situation. You may not land the deciding punch, but God's will shall be done. 2 Timothy 1:7 tells us that "For God hath not given us the spirit of fear; but of power, and of love, and of a sound mind." Have a great day!

Prayer

O God, be with me as face the challenges of this day. If I have to fight, guide me and strengthen me. In Jesus' Name. Amen.

Personal Reflections

Date: _____

Thoughts:_____

_____

_____

_____

_____

_____

_____

This Day's Objective:_____

_____

_____

_____

_____

_____

37. Give Jesus

Acts 3:6 Then Peter said, Silver and gold have I none; but such as I have give I thee: In the name of Jesus Christ of Nazareth rise up and walk.

Week after week, I would go visit persons incarcerated for various reasons. My instructions were to give pastoral care to anyone requesting it. Knowing that the persons who were detained at this facility had committed all types of crimes, I prayed for direction in what to say and do because I didn't know where to start. On the first visit, I was invited to play a game of spades with these individuals and it opened a way to have dialogue. A young man began to share the story of how he had just become a father and he didn't want his son to have to live like he did. He didn't want his son to commit crimes and get locked up in some criminal institution. He had never seen his new born son, but he said he loved his son dearly. Then he began to talk about his family life and how he wasn't a religious person even though his family goes to church. He then asked me to explain this "God thing" to him. So I told him how much God loved humankind. God loved humankind so much that God gave his only son to save them from their sins. Just like prisoner would give anything to see his son have a better life, God loves us even more because he gave his only son who died for our sins. All we have to do is believe and God can do a new thing in our lives. I asked him to think about how much he loved his son. As he thought about it, tears began to fall down his face in the middle of this prison common area with cursing going on all around. I asked him did he understand now. He nodded. From that point on, he always came to hear an encouraging word when I visited. I gave this man a new perspective about this "God thing". In other words, I gave him Jesus without condemning him or putting him down.

As we go through life, we will find many people who just need to see the Jesus in us. Jesus sat down with many sinners. (Matthew 9:10) "And it came to pass, as Jesus sat at meat in the house, behold, many publicans and sinners came and sat down with him and his disciples". We should be able to do the same thing however the only major difference is we are a sinner too. Jesus was without sin. 1 Timothy 1:15 reminds us "This [is] a faithful saying, and worthy of all acceptation, that Christ Jesus came into the world to save sinners; of whom I am chief. " The only Jesus that many people see is the Jesus in you. Give a little Jesus to someone today.

Have a great day!

Prayer

O God, help me to live so that others may see the Jesus in my life. I want to live pleasing to you and as you place people in my space. Let me be a blessing to them. In Jesus' Name. Amen

Personal Reflections

Date: _____

Thoughts:_____

_____

_____

_____

_____

_____

_____

This Day's Objective:_____

_____

_____

_____

_____

_____

_____

_____

38. Serving God No Matter What

Daniel 3:17-18 If it be [so], our God whom we serve is able to deliver us from the burning fiery furnace, and he will deliver [us] out of thine hand, O king. But if not, be it known unto thee, O king, that we will not serve thy gods, nor worship the golden image which thou hast set up.

Throughout the world, what we believe and what God we serve can affect our stature in society, our livelihood, or even our life. Every Monday morning in the United States, billions of people get out of bed and head to some job. Others who may be retired or disabled have plans for their Monday morning as well. Most people will interact with other people at some point throughout the course of the day. How we interact is guided by what we believe and what God we serve. Many people opt for the convenient, politically correct method of serving God which means no public expression of the religious beliefs past Sunday morning.

Yet, many other people find that there is no magical on/off switch for serving God. We serve God 24 hours a day seven days a week. Those who can serve God in spirit and truth can find God in their sunrise, in their breakfast, in the greeting of family members in the morning, in greeting of strangers during the day, in the face of opposition, and even in the feeling of the heat from the sun as you walk outside. Do we just serve God when it seemingly cost nothing to serve God? Dietrich Bonhoeffer, a German theologian born in 1906, speaks of "Cheap Grace": "[It] is the preaching of forgiveness without requiring repentance, baptism without church discipline, Communion without confession, absolution without personal confession. Cheap grace is grace without discipleship, grace without the cross, grace without Jesus Christ, living and incarnate."

In a world where people are killed daily for the God they serve and how they serve their God, are you willing to serve your God no matter what? If you are not at that level, there is room for spiritual and personal growth. Shadrach, Meshak, and Abednego found that when they stood against oppressive forces to serve God, God stood with them. As they were thrown into the fiery furnace, those on the outside witnessed a fourth person walking in the fire with them. God protected them and they came out the fire with no burns or smell of smoke. God is faithful to God's promises to us. We are called to be faithful to God.

Have a great day!

Prayer

O God, help me to have a transparent faith which I grow in when I'm worshipping you on the Sabbath and when live daily in good times and in difficult times. In Jesus' Name. Amen

Personal Reflections

Date: _____

Thoughts:_____

_____

_____

_____

_____

_____

This Day's Objective:_____

_____

_____

_____

_____

_____

_____

39. Fire around and the inside

Zechariah 2:5 For I, saith the LORD, will be unto her a wall of fire round about, and will be the glory in the midst of her.

There was an older African American lady who lived through three wars, the roaring twenties, the great depression of the 40's, and even the turbulent civil rights era of the 60's and 70's. Every time you would see this lady, you would see her smile as she greeted whomever with a "Good Morning", "Good Afternoon", or a "Good Evening". She would always seem to smile at people with this infectious grin that caused the other person to smile back. When she got really excited, she would say "God is good" as she would clap her hands. If you managed to get in a conversation with her, you would find out that she would leave you with a pearl of wisdom like "If you trust God, He will see you through!"

In this verse from Zechariah, he is talking about Jerusalem. In the second chapter, Zechariah says he saw an angel who was talking to a man. The angel told the man that "Jerusalem shall be inhabited [as] towns without walls for the multitude of men and cattle therein:". In other words, Jerusalem will exist as a town without wall according to the naked eye. In the fifth verse, the angel cleared up this wall matter. God will be the wall around Jerusalem and even fill Jerusalem within. That's why David could say in Psalm 23 "Ye though I walk through the valley of the shadow of death, I will fear no evil for thy rod and thy staff comfort me. Thou preparest a table before me in the presence of mine enemies. Thou annoint my head with oil." David knew that God with him was more the world against him. No matter what may go on in the world, God can and God will build a fence around his children. The glory of God will also shine from within his children so you'll know them by how they are. Leviticus 25:17-18 reminds us that "Ye shall not therefore oppress one another; but thou shalt fear thy God: for I [am] the LORD your God. Wherefore ye shall do my statutes, and keep my judgments, and do them; and ye shall dwell in the land in safety." Praise God for the wall of fire around us through this day and the fire within us!!

Have a great day!

Prayer

O God, Thank you for the fire within. Thank for your presence and your protection. I can face this day and life's challenges because you are with me. I can smile and greet those that I meet because of how I experience you. Continue to protect and keep me. In Jesus' Name. Amen.

Personal Reflections

Date: _____

Thoughts:_____

_____

_____

_____

_____

_____

This Day's Objective:_____

_____

_____

_____

_____

_____

_____

_____

40. Heaven

Revelation 21:1-8

There are increasingly more and more questions about what heaven is like and what about the end of time. I don't have an answer for when the end of time will be but I can let the words from the book of Revelation speak to this matter of heaven:

"And I saw a new heaven and a new earth: for the first heaven and the first earth were passed away; and there was no more sea. And I John saw the holy city, new Jerusalem, coming down from God out of heaven, prepared as a bride adorned for her husband. And I heard a great voice out of heaven saying, Behold, the tabernacle of God [is] with men, and he will dwell with them, and they shall be his people, and God himself shall be with them, [and be] their God. And God shall wipe away all tears from their eyes; and there shall be no more death, neither sorrow, nor crying, neither shall there be any more pain: for the former things are passed away. And he that sat upon the throne said, Behold, I make all things new. And he said unto me, Write: for these words are true and faithful. And he said unto me, It is done. I am Alpha and Omega, the beginning and the end. I will give unto him that is athirst of the fountain of the water of life freely. He that overcometh shall inherit all things; and I will be his God, and he shall be my son." (Revelation 21:1-8)

Revelation 22:1-5 also says: *"And he shewed me a pure river of water of life, clear as crystal, proceeding out of the throne of God and of the Lamb. In the midst of the street of it, and on either side of the river, [was there] the tree of life, which bare twelve [manner of] fruits, [and] yielded her fruit every month: and the leaves of the tree [were] for the healing of the nations. And there shall be no more curse: but the throne of God and of the Lamb shall be in it; and his servants shall serve him: And they shall see his face; and his name [shall be] in their foreheads. And there shall be no night there; and they need no candle, neither light of the sun; for the Lord God giveth them light: and they shall reign for ever and ever."*

Much has been written about heaven and there are many biblical references for heaven, but for the believer, three facts remain: There is a heaven. There is a hell. Jesus will return again to reign as King of Kings and Lord of Lords.

Have a great day!

Prayer

O Merciful and Gracious God, which are heaven, hallowed be thy name. Thy kingdom come and thy will be done on earth as it is heaven. For thine is the kingdom, and the power, and the glory forever, Amen.

Personal Reflections

Date: _____

Thoughts:_____

_____

_____

_____

_____

_____

_____

This Day's Objective:_____

_____

_____

_____

_____

_____

_____

_____

41. Christ is Coming Again

Matthew 24:42 Watch therefore: for ye know not what hour your Lord doth come.

During each August or September in cities all over the United States, Pre-Kindergarten and Kindergarten aged children go to school to begin a new school year. The children and their parents experience excitement, nervousness, and even anxiety associated with going to school. The children are told as their parents drop them off for school that they will come again and pick them up that afternoon.   It seems like a simple instruction for adults, but for a child who can't tell time it is an awesome feat. This child meets new students, new teachers, performs new activities, and a myriad of activities through the course of the day. One thing that the child remembers is that their parent will come and pick them up.   The child doesn't know the exact hour or minute, but they look for the signs that it is time for mom, pop, or even grandma to come and pick me up.   They learn to associate it with a bell, a buzzer, or a teacher announcing that it is time to go home.   With those triggers, excitement builds as the child gathers their belongings to go home with their loved one.   Jesus reminds us that as children of God we must be watchful as well.   Jesus promised to return again to take his children home, but we must hold steadfast until he comes.   Some will be living and some will have died in Christ, but the fact remains that at some point in the future the great school bell of life will ring and Christ will descend from the clouds and call his children home to heaven. Matthew 24:37-41 tells us "But as the days of Noe [were], so shall also the coming of the Son of man be. For as in the days that were before the flood they were eating and drinking, marrying and giving in marriage, until the day that Noe entered into the ark, And knew not until the flood came, and took them all away; so shall also the coming of the Son of man be. Then shall two be in the field; the one shall be taken, and the other left. Two [women shall be] grinding at the mill; the one shall be taken, and the other left." Finally, "Therefore be ye also ready: for in such an hour as ye think not the Son of man cometh." (Matthew 24:44)

HAVE A GREAT DAY!

Prayer

O God, Let me not grow weary while waiting on your return. Help me to live in a way that if Jesus returns, I will be caught up to meet Him in the air. And if Jesus does not return in my lifetime, help me live so that you will be pleased with my living. In Jesus' Name. Amen.

Personal Reflections

Date: _____

Thoughts:_____

_____

_____

_____

_____

_____

_____

This Day's Objective:_____

_____

_____

_____

_____

_____

42. Our Heritage

Isaiah 54:17 No weapon that is formed against thee shall prosper; and every tongue [that] shall rise against thee in judgment thou shalt condemn. This [is] the heritage of the servants of the LORD, and their righteousness [is] of me, saith the LORD.

Many people may remember the old band-aid commercial. Any time a child had a bump or bruise called an "owie", the child would get a band-aid to cover it up.   As adults, if we have ills or hurts, we quickly call a doctor or health center to make an appointment. Even if we are broke or have little cash on hand, we pull out our trusty insurance card or Medicare card to make arrangements for payment. In most states, you can not drive a newly purchased car off the car lot without proof of insurance on the vehicle if you are financing the car. The insurance is our and the bank's protection against unforeseen danger. As a human being, as sure as we are born into the world, at some point along way we will encounter trouble. "Man [that is] born of a woman [is] of few days, and full of trouble." (Job 14:1) But as a servant of God or a faithful believer of God, we have some insurance that beats Allstate, State Farm, Mutual of Omaha, and even Metlife. Even though we may encounter trouble, "NO WEAPON that is formed against us shall prosper".   To those that serve God, God promises protection according to God's will.   Job was an upright man. According Job 1:8, "And the LORD said unto Satan, Hast thou considered my servant Job, that [there is] none like him in the earth, a perfect and an upright man, one that feareth God, and escheweth evil?" Job encountered trouble in his home, in his job, on his body, among his friends, and even in the community but he remained faithful to God.   God protected Job through the entire experience and even restored Job with more than he originally started out with. Job 42:12-13 says "So the LORD blessed the latter end of Job more than his beginning: for he had fourteen thousand sheep, and six thousand camels, and a thousand yoke of oxen, and a thousand she asses. He had also seven sons and three daughters." Our heritage as servants of God is to be in the arms of safety of the Most High God.

Have a Great DAY!!!

Prayer

O God, Thank you for being a fence around me protecting me from seen and unseen dangers. Continue protect me from the adversary. In Jesus' Name. Amen

Personal Reflections

Date: _____

Thoughts:_____

_____

_____

_____

_____

_____

_____

This Day's Objective:_____

_____

_____

43. Be A Light on a Hill

Matthew 5:14 Ye are the light of the world. A city that is set on an hill cannot be hid.

Jane went about her day as most people do. She arose every morning, brushed her teeth, put on her clothes, ate breakfast, and started the day. The interesting thing about this woman is that she never spoke to anyone, smiled at anyone, or even shook anyone's hand during the course of the day except on Sunday. Why was Sunday so different? On Sunday, Jane was a deaconess serving on the deaconess board at her church. She wore a white doily on her head, a white dress, white shoes with matching white gloves, and a white "pockie book" or purse. At church she greeted everyone who came within 5 feet of her. She would hug you, kiss you, or shake your hand. Everyone thought Miss Jane as she was affectionately called was the sweetest God fearing woman that ever walked. Yet, during the week "Miss Jane" had nothing to do with people. When she came in contact with other people during the week, she seemed to be cold toward them. As Christians, we are the light of the world. Where there is light darkness can not exist. Another example is a lady who used to keep the offices clean at my place of work. Every time, not sometime, that you would see this kind lady she would greet you, hug you, or even ask how you were doing. She just had a beautiful spirit about her. Every time she would get in the elevator, the mood of the elevator would always brighten. Matthew 5:16 says "Let your light so shine before men, that they may see your good works, and glorify your Father which is in heaven." There are simple ways to let your light shine that used to be common practice in days gone by: when you walk in a room, speak to everyone. If you see someone that you haven't seen, say good morning, good afternoon, or good evening. Shake someone's hand. Smile at someone. Say "Thank You" when someone does something for you. The simple things make GREAT impressions.

Have a great day!

Prayer

O God, Let the spirit of you resonate in my life and out of my life so that everyone that I experience will experience you through me. Let my little light shine. In Jesus' name, Amen.

Personal Reflections

Date: _____

Thoughts:_____

_____

_____

_____

_____

_____

This Day's Objective:_____

_____

_____

_____

_____

_____

_____

44. Baptizing Clean

Numbers 8:7 And thus shalt thou do unto them, to cleanse them: Sprinkle water of purifying upon them, and let them shave all their flesh, and let them wash their clothes, and [so] make themselves clean.

Most people like cleanliness. We purchase laundry detergent, bleach, and even fabric softener to make our clothes smell fresh when we wear them. We purchase dish detergent to clean our dishes. We purchase auto cleaner to make the car or truck shine like new. We even purchase all types of soaps and moisturizers to make our bodies smell fresh. Of course, we have to keep washing to stay fresh or use deodorant or perfume to make the good smell last longer. As time goes on, our bodies naturally produce odors that we have to go back and clean again. Fortunately, our souls can be cleansed as well. Our souls are made unclean by sin. Even before Jesus came, God's children saw a need to clean themselves and we see this example of cleansing and purifying in Numbers 8:7. Water was sprinkled on them to cleanse them. Secondly, after Jesus came, John cleansed by way of baptism in river. (Matthew 3:11) "I indeed baptize you with water unto repentance: but he that cometh after me is mightier than I, whose shoes I am not worthy to bear: he shall baptize you with the Holy Ghost, and [with] fire: " Jesus is able to cleanse us with the Holy Spirit. In our effort to become clean, we must allow the baptism of the holy spirit to take place. Water can only do so much but the Holy Spirit can perform with "deep cleansing action". We must say as David said, "Create in me a clean heart,

O God; and renew a right spirit within me." (Psalm 51:10) Have a great day!

Prayer

God, create in me a clean heart, O God; and renew the right spirit within me. Cast me not away from thy presence. Take not thy Holy Spirit from me. Amen

Personal Reflections

Date: _____

Thoughts:_____

_____

_____

_____

_____

This Day's Objective:_____

_____

_____

_____

_____

_____

45. Faithful Prayer

Mark 11:22-24 And Jesus answering saith unto them, Have faith in God. For verily I say unto you, That whosoever shall say unto this mountain, Be thou removed, and be thou cast into the sea; and shall not doubt in his heart, but shall believe that those things which he saith shall come to pass; he shall have whatsoever he saith. Therefore I say unto you, What things soever ye desire, when ye pray, believe that ye receive [them], and ye shall have [them].

Activated faith is one of the most powerful weapons that the child of God has in their arsenal. Activated faith will cause a lil ruddy sheep herder to grab a few smooth stones and walk in front of a well armed army to slay a giant with only one stone. Activated faith will cause a an indebted, poor, widowed woman to give the only thing she has, a little oil, to a prophet who takes her faith action and pours oil into every empty container that she can gather up. When every container is full, there is a enough oil to sell in order for her and her son to pay their bills and live. Activated faith will cause a prophet to wage a war on a city by walking around the city walls seven times and shouting at the end to celebrate the victory while watching the walls come tumbling down. Activated faith will cause a crippled person to take up their bed and walk.   Activated faith is also relevant to prayer. You must trust in God and believe that God will answer your prayer.   Ask for what you want and believe God will hear your prayer. Even in the Lord's Prayer, watch God answer that simple prayer with your daily bread, forgiveness, direction, and much more. Activated faith doesn't stop with your asking God what you want. Activated faith continues with expectation of an answer. If you ask for rain, you better find your umbrella. If you ask for increase in finances, you better get your check book ready. Finally, be thankful and praise God for what is about to happen. God inhabits the praise of his people and delights in those who are grateful. Lord bless this person reading this to grow in faith as they pray to you.

Have a great day!

Prayer

O God, hear my prayer. Meet my needs. Thanks for all you have done, all you are doing, and all you are going to do. Help me to be patient as you answer my prayer. Help me to experience your answer. In Jesus' Name. Amen.

Personal Reflections

Date: _____

Thoughts:_____

_____

_____

_____

_____

This Day's Objective:_____

_____

_____

_____

_____

_____

_____

46. Alive to Praise God

Isaiah 38:18-19 For the grave cannot praise thee, death can [not] celebrate thee: they that go down into the pit cannot hope for thy truth. The living, the living, he shall praise thee, as I [do] this day: the father to the children shall make known thy truth.

During most funerals, one of the most interesting portions of some funeral services is the "reflections" section.   During this section, loved ones, friends, family, and whomever stand in front of the assembly to discuss their impressions and memories of the deceased person in question. Most of these are intended to praise the individual lying in the coffin if possible. At one funeral or home going service of this particular man, a lady rose with a cane and proceeded to the front of the church next to the coffin. She then turned around and said "He was a good man. He sure could cuss. As a matter of fact you ain't heard cussing till you heard him cuss. He could cuss you with words you ain't never heard before. To his widow, I will say "you keep a keepin on and God will see you through". At this time, the widow grimaced but forced a smile to come out. It was one of those smiles that said, "Old lady, I think you need to sit down!" While this old lady's words might not have been the most appropriate, regardless of what is said at the funeral, it can't help or hurt the person lying in coffin with respect to how they lived their life or the state of their salvation. Those of us living are given the breath of life to give honor, glory, and adoration to the giver of life. "The LORD God formed man [of] the dust of the ground, and breathed into his nostrils the breath of life; and man became a living soul."(Genesis 2:7) Since we humans have breath, "Let every thing that hath breath praise the LORD. Praise ye the LORD." (Psalm 150:6) Just as praise at a funeral can't help a person lying in a casket, if a person is a dead, it's too late for them to praise God. As Isaiah so eloquently points out, from the grave, we can't praise God simply because the breath of life is absent from the body. So if you are breathing, you need to allow some of that breath to utter praise unto God not simply for what God has done but for WHO god is. Who is God to you? When God was asked about his name, God said tell them my name is "I am". God was letting us know that God is so many things that they can't name them all here: Jehovah Jireh (God our provider), Jehova Nissi (God my banner),Jehovah Ropehka (God heals thee), Jehovah Shalom (God who sends peace), Jehovah Shammah (God is there), and the list goes on. Now, if you are breathing, do you have praise for God? How about the highest praise, Hallelujah!

Have a great day!

Prayer

O God,
I praise you for who you are to me, my provider, my peace, my banner, my healer, my everything. Hallelujah! Amen

Personal Reflections

Date: _____

Thoughts:_____

_____

_____

_____

_____

_____

_____

This Day's Objective:_____

_____

_____

_____

_____

_____

_____

_____

47. Righteous Boldness

2 Timothy 1:7 For God hath not given us the spirit of fear; but of power, and of love, and of a sound mind.

In 1892, Homer Adolph Plessy was a thirty two year old resident of New Orleans who was considered 1/8 Black by standard practices of that era although his skin tone was light enough to pass for a white person. Louisiana had enacted a Separate Car act which required segregation when riding the railroad.   Mr. Plessy boldly purchased a first class ticket on a train to Covington, Louisiana and took a seat in the "whites only" section. After he told the conductor that he was 1/8 Black, he was arrested and his case went to trial. In 1896, the Plessy vs. Ferguson case was heard by the United States Supreme Court which sanctioned the "Separate but Equal" doctrine that ruled this country for almost 50 years. The decision was finally struck down in 1954 in the Brown vs. Board of Education case. Even Rosa Parks, in 1954, boldly refused to give up her seat during a period in Alabama history where segregation flourished. While the forces of segregation and racism flourished during that time in American history, a few people dared to face injustice in the face. Moses boldly faced Pharaoh on behalf of the children of Israel even though he had a speech impediment. Even Jesus, faced the leaders of the day, to speak of justice, mercy, and love. As you face life's challenges, be strong in the Lord by power of His might. (Ephesians 6:10) Face the challenges squarely in the face with prayer, love, and righteousness. Face your children with boldness, your job with boldness, you friends and associates with boldness, and the world with boldness. Look for great things to happen.

Have a great day!

Prayer

O God, thank you being with me to face this day. Help me to boldly be a person you have designed me to be this day in a way that is pleasing to you. In Jesus' Name. Amen

Personal Reflections

Date: _____

Thoughts:_____
_____
_____
_____
_____
_____

This Day's Objective:_____
_____
_____
_____
_____
_____
_____

48. People at the Pool

John 5:8 Jesus saith unto him, Rise, take up thy bed, and walk.

One of America's treasures is its transit system. You can travel by car on the mass, complex interstate highway system. You can travel by airplane to almost any point in the world. One less used mode of travel is the bus line service. For usually under a $100, you can travel to many places across the country. While sitting in the bus station waiting on my bus to arrive, I had an opportunity to observe life in a bus terminal. It was unlike that of a train station or even an airport. There were persons lying on the floor attempting to sleep. There were many people who were there because of their economic situations. Others were there because they felt safer riding a bus rather than an airplane. I also saw several drug dealers, some pan handlers, some college students, and some persons who looked like they had no where else to go. For example, there was a Caucasian lady in her late 20's who wore headset and danced from one end of the bus terminal to the other end doing dips, leg lifts, and many other dance moves. Some people gave this lady money as she danced. Most of us were there to travel, but some were there to survive. This reminded me of the pool of Bethesda mentioned in John 5:1-8. According to the text, this pool located in Jerusalem, contained "a great multitude of impotent folk, of blind, halt, withered, waiting for the moving of the water. For an angel went down at a certain season into the pool, and troubled the water: whosoever then first after the troubling of the water stepped in was made whole of whatsoever disease he had." (John 5:3-4) There was a man who had been sick for 38 years. Jesus asked the man, "Will you be made whole?" Jesus wanted to know what the man thought about his infirmity. It's one thing to be sick and think you're going to get well and it's another to be sick and not desire to get well. The man replied that he had no one to put him in the water which was not really a good answer to what Jesus was asking. Jesus, then challenged the man by saying, "Rise, take up thy bed, and walk." It's about faith and hope. We go to and fro every day with people all around us doing their thing. Are we waiting for someone to place us in the pool of our blessing or will we do as Jesus asked the man to do by rising up and stepping into what God has for us? At this bus station, some people got up and got on the bus to their intended destinations. Others waited around for someone to bring a blessing to them. What are you doing at your pool? Rise up, take up your bed, and walk.

Have a great day!

Prayer

O God, I thank you for your grace and your mercy shone to me this day. Help me to face the challenges of this day. As I move through this day, guide me to the place where you desire to me bed. I believe you will guide me all the way. In Jesus' Name. Amen.

Personal Reflections

Date: _____

Thoughts:_____

_____

_____

_____

_____

_____

_____

This Day's Objective:_____

_____

_____

_____

_____

_____

_____

_____

49. Old and Young to Advance a People

Proverbs 20:29 The glory of young men [is] their strength: and the beauty of old men [is] the gray head.

Dr. Maya Angelou says in her Black Family Pledge, "BECAUSE we have forgotten our ancestors, our children no longer give us honor. BECAUSE we have lost the path our ancestors cleared kneeling in perilous undergrowth, our children cannot find their way. BECAUSE we have banished the God of our ancestors, our children cannot pray. BECAUSE the old wails of our ancestors have faded beyond our hearing, our children cannot hear us crying." The prophet Joel says in verse 1:3 of the book of Joel to "Tell ye your children of it, and [let] your children [tell] their children, and their children another generation." What we do directly affects how our children interpret the world. If we have little respect for our elders, then our children may learn to disrespect authority. If elders have condescending attitudes toward the young, prosperity is stifled. Old women can teach a girl how to become a woman while an old man can teach a boy how to become a man. A young girl can remind an old woman of what she may have forgotten. In order for this happen, the two must be in dialogue. The young have strength and stamina to run the way, but the old know the way. If both work together, an entire people can move through the way beyond the way. I can remember my dad saying things like racism is learned. Then he'd say, "what color is this dollar bill? Is it black or white?" I'd say that it was green. Or I heard my grandmother say things like "Don't run in packs because packs can lead you astray. Learn to think on your own." Or mother would say things like "you need to keep things clean. It will make you feel better." At the same time, they would listen to what I had to say. For a people to advance there are two essential elements: the young and the old. The two don't exist in vacuums and for the optimum outcome both should connect at points. Yes, let the old be old and the young be young, but don't let generational differences stifle progress. Both are important.

Have a Great Day!

Prayer
Dear God, Thanks for my elders, my ancestors, and all those who have come before me. Help me to relate to my elders as well as the generations that follow me. Help us be as you would have us to be. In Jesus' Name. Amen.

Personal Reflections

Date: _____

Thoughts:_____

_____

_____

_____

_____

_____

_____

This Day's Objective:_____

_____

_____

_____

_____

_____

_____

50. A Dose of Laughter

Proverbs 17:22 A merry heart doeth good [like] a medicine: but a broken spirit drieth the bones.

In the coldness of winter, we would make a fire in the fireplace at my grandmother's house. While there was a television and a radio in the house, no one really watched either. We'd either find a chair or sit on the floor around the fireplace. An extra special treat would be a bucket full of pecans. As we'd crack, shell, and eat pecans, the stories would begin. For example, there was a story of how my grandfather sold moonshine to the local town's people. It was so good that people would come from miles around to buy this corn liquor. At some point, a goat fell over into the still and got cooked with the corn mash. They finished making the corn liquor and bottled it up. People who bought that batch of liquor said it was the best 'shine that they had tasted. As this portion of the story was told, there would be big bursts of laughter. The stories and the laughter would continue over into the night until we got sleepy. While we were not the richest people, we were happy. While we didn't have the finest material things in life, we were happy. While we didn't have luxury cars, gold, diamonds, or even silver, we were happy. We didn't think about the things we didn't have. We thought about the times with each other. When we couldn't find something else to laugh at, we'd laugh at ourselves. People in the community would come by and visit just to sit and laugh. Stories and laughter provided the best medicine to face a world which at that time was facing gas shortages, discrimination, killing, pestilence, and a long laundry list of societal ills. In our moment around the fireplace, we found some of the best therapy for facing life's challenges. We found laughter. If you're having a tough day, find something to laugh about. Look at yourself and don't take yourself too serious. Now, doesn't that feel better?

Have a great day!

Prayer

God, thank you for your laughter. Help me not to take myself to serious. Amen

134

Personal Reflections

Date: _____

Thoughts:_____

_____

_____

_____

_____

_____

This Day's Objective:_____

_____

_____

_____

_____

_____

_____

51. Teaching and Healing in the Synagogue

Luke 13:10-13 And he (Jesus) was teaching in one of the synagogues on the sabbath. And, behold, there was a woman which had a spirit of infirmity eighteen years, and was bowed together, and could in no wise lift up [herself]. And when Jesus saw her, he called [her to him], and said unto her, Woman, thou art loosed from thine infirmity. And he laid [his] hands on her: and immediately she was made straight, and glorified God.

With the advent of radio and now television and internet, evangelists have been using media to deliver the message of the gospel since as early as the 1930's. Other Countries around the world have even followed pursuit in this form of ministry. There have been well noted evangelists such Billy Graham, Jerry Falwell, Pat Robertson, Eddie Long, T.D. Jakes, and Joel Osteen, Tammy Faye Bakker, Rev. Leroy Jenkins, Joyce Myers, and even Rev. Ike who is well known for his saying of "You can't loose with the stuff I use." With this development of televangelism, many people have taken the position that I don't have to go to church. Why go? I can have church right in my bed, my sofa, my living room or my kitchen. While God can meet you any where that God wants to meet you, there is something special about going to the church. Some stop going to a particular church because of confusion like the confusion talked about in Acts 19:32. It just takes at least two or three to assemble in God's name for God to dwell in the midst.(Matthew 18:20). This Lukan text speaks to two great things that happened at the synagogue or the church: one is teaching and the second is healing. At the tabernacle, at the church, at the synagogue, the scripture is proclaimed, prayers are lifted, exhortation is performed, and basically, teaching takes place. Jesus illumines the mind in the church and secondly there is healing that takes place. This text says that upon being healed, this woman immediately stood up. God can make wondrous things happen anywhere, but if you find your way to the church, expect God to do something. If we say we are Christians, we are not isolated because we belong to the body of Christ. "But if we walk in the light, as he is in the light, we have fellowship one with another, and the blood of Jesus Christ his Son cleanseth us from all sin." (1 John 1:7) Some may think they are in fellowship over the telephone, but there is nothing like being in fellowship in the presence with other believers. Go to church and expect something great.

Have a great day!

Prayer

God, who created heaven and earth, thank you. Lead me to a place of worship where I can experience you, worship you, be taught, be healed, and experience the fellowship of other believers. Amen

Personal Reflections

Date: _____

Thoughts:_____

_____

_____

_____

_____

_____

_____

This Day's Objective:_____

_____

_____

_____

_____

_____

_____

52. Never Alone

John 14:16 "And I will pray the Father, and he shall give you another Comforter, that he may abide with you for ever;"

Guess what? You're never alone. Jesus prayed that you will forever have a comforter. If Jesus asked on our behalf, I'm inclined to believe that God, the father, heard him and answered him. You should too!

Have a great day!

Prayer

God, thank you for never leaving me and being always with me. In Jesus' Name. Amen.

Personal Reflections

Date: _____

Thoughts:_____

_____

_____

_____

_____

_____

This Day's Objective:_____

_____

_____

_____

_____

_____

_____

53. A Good Word

Proverbs 12:25 Heaviness in the heart of man maketh it stoop: but a good word maketh it glad.

In watching News broadcasts across the country, there is so much to make people's hearts heavy. There are stories of killing, deceit, deception, lies, distrust, infidelity, and more. Rarely do you hear of good news. It's no surprise that so many people are experiencing trouble in their families, their relationships, and their day to day livelihood. We are force fed negativity from around the world. "The enemy comes to kill, steal, and destroy," but Christ comes that we may have life and have it more abundantly. We do need to know what is going on in our world so that we can be good stewards over what God has blessed us with, however we need to feed our spirits some "good spiritual" food. Read good books, good articles, or good stories. Listen to good messages, good songs, good poems, and good speeches. Watch good movies, good television programs, good plays, and good events. Take time to give the people you love a good word. If you want to lift a person, feed them a good word.

Have a great day!

Prayer

God, Thank you for your word. Thank you for the ability to encourage myself and to encourage others. Help me to be light every where I go. In Jesus' Name. Amen.

Personal Reflections

Date: _____

Thoughts:_____

_____

_____

_____

_____

_____

This Day's Objective:_____

_____

_____

_____

_____

_____

_____

54. Double Minded People

James 1:8 A double minded man [is] unstable in all his ways.

There was a little old lady who was the vision of meekness and grace. She wore stately hats and gloves to church as she would sit on the second row pew on the left side of church every Sunday.   She had a shiny gold tooth on her top dentures that would glisten as she smiled at people as they walked by her. One Sunday, she invited me to join her and her family for dinner after church and I, seeing no threat, gladly accepted--especially since the woman was known for baking skills. As I entered her house, sitting in the living room, there was the pastor of the church and his wife and her nieces and grandchildren. We ate a bountiful dinner majestically served on China and silver service ware. The pastor left shortly after dinner, and then the woman changed from the smiling gentle lady to a cussing, bitter woman. She said, "the pastor tried eat up all her damn food!" As I listened to the many things she said, this woman although pleasant in most situations was also a very bitter woman. If she said this about the pastor while he was getting into his vehicle, I can only imagine what she said about me after I left. Nevertheless, it pointed out a very important lesson: Watch a dog who brings a bone to you. He'll also carry one away. In other words, people who tell you mean and malicious things about some people will say mean and malicious things about you. People who are one way one minute and another way the next minute are very unstable. It is so easy to posture for a particular situation and change for another. James reminds us that these people are unstable and we should be careful of them. We should still love them because they are still children of God, but for our own good and welfare, be cautious. Treasure the people who have integrity. They are the same no matter when you see them. HAVE A GREAT DAY!

Prayer

God, Give me the ability to discern double minded people. Help me to be cautious when dealing with them. Secondly, help me to be a person of integrity. Keep me from being a double minded person. In Jesus' Name. Amen.

Personal Reflections

Date: _____

Thoughts:_____
_____
_____
_____
_____
_____
_____

This Day's Objective:_____
_____
_____
_____
_____
_____
_____

55. Things Work Together

Romans 8:28 And we know that all things work together for good to them that love God, to them who are the called according to [his] purpose.

There is a saying which says "Plan your work and work your plan." For the typical person who is going on a trip, they do things to prepare for the trip such as purchasing a ticket on a plane or bus or choosing to drive their own vehicle. As a little boy when preparing to go on a long trip, my mom would get up early in the morning and fry some chicken and wrap it in aluminum foil. There would also be some carbonated drink wrapped in foil along with a few slices of bread. Therefore when hunger came, I had something to eat in my brown paper bag. We try to prepare for things that come our way but we can't always see everything that is coming, but God does. While it is good to prepare, we must also trust God to provide--Jehovah Jireh. Once I received a speeding citation for $450 from a small town in south Georgia. I refused to pay it without going to court. I went to court and signed in that morning and took at seat about 8:00 a.m. The judge heard and processed case after case throughout the morning. Most people were paying $600 for speeding citations. I prayed for God to move in this situation because I only had $300 cash in my pocket. At 12:00 p.m., the judge said that the court was dismissed for lunch. He then looked at me and said "Son, what are you here for?" I said, "I am here for a speeding citation". He instructed me to see the district attorney. The district attorney asked me if I had been to the town before, I said, "No." He said, "Since you have been sitting here all morning, what

can we work out for you? What can you pay? Can
you pay $250?" Trying to contain the excitement, I
said, "YES!". He said "What if I reduce this speed on
this ticket so you won't get any points?" I gladly
obliged. I paid the $250 and had enough to have
lunch afterward.   All things work together for the
good of those who love the Lord and are called
according to His purpose. Do the right thing and let
God do God's thing!

Have a great day!

Prayer

*God, give me patience to allow you to work in my life.
While I may not understand everything going on and
why it happens the way it does, I will trust you to
make it all work for my good. In Jesus' Name. Amen.*

Personal Reflections

Date: _____

Thoughts:_____

_____

_____

_____

_____

_____

This Day's Objective:_____

_____

_____

_____

_____

_____

_____

_____

56. Joy in a sinner's salvation

Luke 15:2,10 And the Pharisees and scribes murmured, saying, This man receiveth sinners, and eateth with them...Likewise, I say unto you, there is joy in the presence of the angels of God over one sinner that repenteth.

At a first glance, the picture on Sunday morning looks like a picture of pure holiness and perfection. In that picture you see women wearing beautiful white dresses with matching gloves and hats. The gray haired men sitting in the front on the side of the church look like unfettered, irreproachable living landmarks of wisdom dressed very neatly in gray, black, and navy blue suits accented with colorful ties and shiny black shoes. The choir stand is full of people with smiles and joyful expressions on their face as they adorn their stately choir robes. The ushers on the door dressed in black accented with white gloves greet each person with a smile as they enter the sanctuary for the morning worship service. Yet, when a known prostitute, a lady dressed in a mini-skirt, "flip-flaps", uncombed hair, and a very revealing shirt attempts to enter the sanctuary of "God's House", the "Tabernacle", namely the Church, she is quickly escorted to the back pew of the church. The choir turns their attention to this person sitting on the last pew as each of the ladies dressed in white turn around, one-by-one, to look at this lady who has just entered their respectable, proper sanctuary. The pastor recognizing what is happening stands and exhorts to the congregation, "I was glad when they said unto me LET US GO INTO THE HOUSE OF THE LORD". He remembers that one of the white haired gentlemen is a recovered alcoholic; he says ""I was glad when they said unto me LET US GO INTO THE HOUSE OF THE LORD". He then remembers that one of the ladies dressed in white who had been living with one of the white haired gentlemen for 20 years had just gotten married two years prior, he said "I was glad when they said unto me LET US GO INTO THE HOUSE OF THE LORD". He then remembered one of the choir members had just gotten paroled from prison six months prior, he said "I was glad when they said unto me LET US GO INTO THE HOUSE OF THE LORD". He even remembered how God had saved him, he said "I was glad when they said unto me LET US GO INTO THE HOUSE OF THE LORD."

As perfect as we might want to think we are, Isaiah 64:6 reminds us that "But we are all as an unclean [thing], and all our righteousnesses [are] as filthy rags; and we all do fade as a leaf; and our iniquities, like the wind, have taken us away. Yet, with God's grace and mercy, Isaiah 64:8 affirms that "O LORD, thou [art] our father; we [are] the clay, and thou our potter; and we all [are] the work of thy hand." In other words, we are what we are because of the grace of God, therefore its easy to see why Jesus spent time with sinners so that sinners would have an opportunity to be made whole. The pastor remembered that the church was a hospital for sinners through prayers and God's power, old things are become new. (John 3:16) For God so loved the world, that he gave his only begotten Son, that whosoever believeth in him should not perish, but have everlasting life. Angels rejoice over the one that comes to God in repentance. Be a witness where you are so that others will see the light of Jesus in you. Someone may be trying to find their way out of darkness right where you are. The best sermon is the one that other see in you.

Have a Great Day!

Prayer

God, I am a sinner. I believe in the saving power of Jesus' blood. I recognize Jesus Christ as my Lord and Savior. Thank you for saving me. Amen

Personal Reflections

Date: _____

Thoughts:_____

_____

_____

_____

_____

_____

This Day's Objective:_____

_____

_____

_____

_____

_____

_____

57. Wash Day

Psalm 51:2 Wash me throughly from mine iniquity, and cleanse me from my sin.

In the south as with many places around the country, there is a weekly ritual called Wash Day whereby all the dirty clothes within the house are gathered up and washed. I can remember one process was to go clean this huge black pot that could hold about 15-20 gallons of water. This pot was placed on some bricks as wood was strategically placed under the pot to burn. Once the fire was set, water was then toted (a country word for "carried") with buckets from the barrel which caught rain water from the corners of house during rain storms. The water was placed in the pot and heated. Some type of cleaning solution such as soap powder but more commonly lye soap and bleach was put in the pot and the clothes were cooked, rinsed, and then wrung dry through two rolling pins that spun very closely together leaving only enough room to place the wet clothes between them. Only then were the clothes ready to shake and then hang on a clothesline to dry. There was nothing like the smell of fresh clean clothes drying in the wind. When Roman 3:23 tells us that all have sinned and come short of the glory of god, how can we be cleansed without some cleaning? Hebrew 12:27-29 tells us that those things shaken can be removed so the things unshaken can remain. Similarly, the kingdom of God can not be shaken or moved, so let us serve God "acceptably with reverence and godly fear: for our God is a consuming fire." Yes, the wages of sin is death and the gift of god is eternal life through Jesus Christ.(Romans 6:23). We should praise God for the redeeming blood of Jesus which is expiation for our sins, but let us not forget that wash day may include so fire, some water, some cooking, some wringing, some rinsing, and even some drying. We do have a promise in 1 John 1:7 that "if we walk in the light, as he is in the light, we have fellowship one with another, and the blood of Jesus Christ his Son cleanseth us from all sin." Don't you just love wash day!!!

Have a great day!

Prayer

God, Thank you for the redeeming blood of Jesus Christ which washes away my sin. Thank Jesus, for being my Lord and Savior. Amen

Personal Reflections

Date: _____

Thoughts:_____

_____

_____

_____

_____

_____

This Day's Objective:_____

_____

_____

_____

_____

_____

_____

58. Your Decision

Isaiah 6:8 Also I heard the voice of the Lord, saying, Whom shall I send, and who will go for us? Then said I, Here [am] I; send me.

On July 19, 2006, the USA TODAY newspaper reported in an article, "In Tim Ryan's family, he is the addict" that "Addiction is endemic in American families. A USA TODAY/HBO nationwide poll of adults April 27-May 31 found that one in five said they had an immediate relative who at some point had been addicted to alcohol or drugs. That translates into roughly 40 million American adults with a spouse, parent, sibling or child battling addiction. And that doesn't count the millions of children living with an addicted parent." There are all types of addiction such as alcohol, drugs, sex, and many other forms. Ignoring them or not dealing with them hasn't made any of them go away. A decision has to be made who will spend their lives treating people with addictions and someone has to make the decision to get treated. The same applies for many vocations such as accounting, medicine, the clergy, law, musical artists, and many more. Everyone has something that they can do in their lifetime. As a young lad, I used to hear adults say you need to go to school in order to get a good job. While that is true that education does affect one's ability to be placed in the workforce, the end is not to simply get a job. The key is making the decision to walk in your destiny. What is it that God desires you to do or to be? Isaiah stopped to hear the word of the Lord saying that something needs to be done. Isaiah saw the pursuit of that vocation as his calling or the thing that fit him best so he answered "Here am I; send me". With the affect on the family by addiction and release of the USA Today article, someone, hopefully, is saying "Here am I. Send me. I will tackle the issue of addiction." Someone else might say, "Here am I. Send me. I will preach to sinners the liberating Gospel of Jesus Christ." Someone else might say, "Here am I. Send me. I will teach people how to exercise and eat right so that they may be healthy." Someone else might say, "Here am I. Send me. I will open a business providing a service to my community." What is it that God is speaking to you to do? How long will it take you to hear it? Then, what is your decision?

Have a great day!

Prayer

God, Show me what I must do. Here I am. Send me. I will go. In Jesus' Name. Amen.

Personal Reflections

Date: _____

Thoughts:_____

_____

_____

_____

_____

This Day's Objective:_____

_____

_____

_____

_____

_____

59. Ask for What You Want

Luke 11:9-12 And I say unto you, Ask, and it shall be given you; seek, and ye shall find; knock, and it shall be opened unto you. For every one that asketh receiveth; and he that seeketh findeth; and to him that knocketh it shall be opened. If a son shall ask bread of any of you that is a father, will he give him a stone? or if [he ask] a fish, will he for a fish give him a serpent? Or if he shall ask an egg, will he offer him a scorpion?

Babies really can't talk even though they find ways of communicating. A certain cry means "I'm hungry" another cry means "I'm sleepy or someone needs to change my diaper." The list goes on and on but the baby learns to communicate by associating certain sounds with actions that they want. The caregiver has to try to figure out what the baby is wanting. As humans, God does know the desires of our heart, but we are charged to ask for what we want. Ask God for what you need and even what you want. Psalm 37:4 reminds us that we can have what we want as well: "Delight thyself also in the LORD; and he shall give thee the desires of thine heart." Therefore if you want a Mercedes, ask for one, but remember that when you get one it requires more than Ford Escort or a Nissan Sentra. Be careful for what you ask, but definitely ask for what you need.

Have a great day!

Prayer

God, Hear my prayer. Bless me with the desires of my heart. Bless others. In Jesus' Name. Amen.

Personal Reflections

Date: _____

Thoughts:_____

_____

_____

_____

_____

This Day's Objective:_____

_____

_____

_____

_____

_____

_____

60. Music that Breaks Yokes

1 Samuel 16:23 And it came to pass, when the [evil] spirit from God was upon Saul, that David took an harp, and played with his hand: so Saul was refreshed, and was well, and the evil spirit departed from him.

In most cities, there is wide selection of music to choose from on the radio. If you don't want to listen to the radio, you can listen to CD's or even IPOD's. Cell phones now have the ability to download music for listening pleasure. Music is very much a part of most modern day living, however I can remember my grandmother who owned a television and a radio making use of music in the course of the day. As you'd smell bacon cooking in the morning, you would also hear someone humming as the pots were rattling. Sometimes you would hear, "nearer my God to thee, nearer to thee..." or you might hear "by and by when the morning comes..." Music has the ability to break the yokes of pain, of grief, of danger, of fear, and much more. This biblical account from Samuel reminds us that music can make evil spirits leave. It's no surprise that music is very much a part of a worship services along with other daily activities. Some even find that their work days go much quicker and easier as they play music. Personally, I find that inspirational music helps keep evil spirits to a manageable level on job sites. I can say that because I remember what it was like before I started playing inspirational music at my desk and after I started playing the music. Many times a song can speak where someone's talking might not be heard. For example, the hymn, "Someday" has the words,

"Beams of heaven as I go through this wilderness below. Guide my feet in peaceful ways. Turn my midnight into day. When in darkness I would grope, faith always sees a ray of hope. Then go home from life's grief and danger, I shall be free some day. I don't know how long 'twil be or what the future holds for me. But as long as Jesus goes with me I shall be free some day." There are countless other songs that speak to our current position or status in life. What is a song that speaks to your spirit? Let some music sooth your spirit today.

Have a great day!

Prayer

God, Thank you for soothing music. Continue to inspire me and bring peace through music. Amen

Personal Reflections

Date: _____

Thoughts:_____

_____

_____

_____

_____

_____

This Day's Objective:_____

_____

_____

_____

_____

_____

_____

INDEX

161

W